Library of
Davidson College

PEIRCE'S CONCEPTION OF GOD
A Developmental Study

DONNA M. ORANGE

PEIRCE STUDIES

NUMBER 2

10 September 1984
INSTITUTE FOR STUDIES IN PRAGMATICISM
Lubbock, Texas USA 79409

Copyright 1984 by Donna M. Orange
All rights reserved

Library of Congress catalog number: 84 - 080516
ISBN: 0 - 936842 - 02 - 4

Peirce Studies is an irregular monographic serial published by the Institute for Studies in Pragmaticism, Texas Tech University, Lubbock, Texas 79409. All correspondence pertaining to the series should be addressed to K.L. Ketner, Institute Director.

Contents

	INTRODUCTION	vi
I	THE PRE-1867 WRITINGS	1
	Early Influences	
	Kant and Mansel	
	More Early Influences	
	Cambridge High School Lecture of 1863	
	Positivism and the Logic of Science	
II	THE MIDDLE PERIOD: FROM DESIGN TO DEVELOPMENT	25
	1867-1878	
	The Order of Nature	
	Royce's Religious Aspect of Philosophy *(1885)*	
	Other Pre-Milford Writings	
III	THE EARLY ARISBE YEARS	40
	1890-1894	
	1896-1900	
	The Reasonable One	
IV	THE FINAL OPINION (1900-1914)	58
	Royce and Peirce	
	1903 Harvard Lectures	
	Anthropomorphism and Theism	
	1908-1914	
	God or Reason	
V	REASONABLENESS	84
	Peirce's Conception of God	
	Development	
	God and Peirce's Philosophy	
	Critical Assessment	
	REFERENCES	95

ABBREVIATIONS

CP *Collected Papers of Charles Sanders Peirce.* Cambridge: Harvard University Press, 1935, 1958. References are by volume and paragraph number.

NEM *The New Elements of Mathematics by Charles S. Peirce,* ed. C. Eisele. Mouton: The Hague, 1976. References are by volume and page number.

MS *The Charles S. Peirce Papers.* Cambridge: Harvard University Library, Photographic Service, 1966. References follow the numbers in *Annotated Catalogue of the Papers of Charles S. Peirce,* by R. S. Robin, Amherst: University of Massachusetts Press, 1967.

N *Charles Sanders Peirce: Contributions to the Nation,* ed. K. L. Ketner and J. E. Cook, Graduate Studies, Lubbock, Texas: Texas Tech University, 1975-1979, in three volumes. Reference is by volume and page number.

SS *Semiotic and Significs: The Correspondence between Charles S. Peirce and Victoria Lady Welby,* ed. C. S. Hardwick. Bloomington: Indiana University Press, 1977.

INTRODUCTION

> "The only desirable object which is quite satisfactory in itself without any ulterior reason for desiring it, is the reasonable itself."
> (CP 8.140)

From time to time students and friends ask me whether I believe in God. I always respond by asking what sort of God they have in mind. My answer depends on theirs. Similarly, Charles Sanders Peirce (1839-1914) asked himself throughout his life what kind of deity he could find believable. I am intrigued by the attention Peirce, an "exact logician," devoted to this question, and have therefore assembled, roughly in chronological order, from manuscripts and published writings, his remarks on the reality and nature of God. I also wanted to see whether his interest in these questions was casual or temporary, and whether his scientific philosophy and religious thought were so insulated from each other that he could be accused of believing in two truths.

My reading of Peirce has convinced me that his conception of God developed in close connection with the rest of his thought: his realism, his theory of categories, his understanding of logic as semiotic or sign-theory. I am also convinced that religious questions were on Peirce's mind throughout his philosophical career, and that the pragmaticistic-Hegelian answers he found to these questions constitute a major contribution to the twentieth century discussion of the cognitive import of religious language. Readers of this study will have to judge for themselves whether the evidence I display supports these conclusions.

My study is addressed, first of all, to students and readers of Peirce, and does not, as a result, contain detailed explanations of his major philosophical views, which are, thankfully, coming to be better known. The concentrated efforts of the Peirce Edition Project in Indianapolis, of the Institute for Studies in Pragmaticism in Lubbock, and of Carolyn Eisele are making Peirce's work available to scholars and to all interested persons. In addition, the current interest in semiotic is stimulating the study of Peirce by literary critics and other scholars.

My study also attempts to add to this interest by addressing all people who want to reconsider and refine their religious views. I often find people who question or reject traditional theism attracted to what I tell them of Peirce's ideas. They become aware, perhaps for the first time, that there *are* alternative religious conceptions of reality, not just *one* which must be accepted without question, or rejected as childish or unscientific. My book invites people to continue their search for an intellectually satisfying faith, or to reject such a search after having engaged in it with a great philosopher. If my explanations of important Peircean notions sometimes seem too terse for these readers, I hope they will feel impelled to consult Peirce's own writings.

Those readers whose major interest in Peirce is in his science and mathematics may find themselves disappointed that I did not discuss in more detail the relationship of his religious conceptions to his mathematical ideas of continuity, absolutes, infinity, and so on. I can only reply that while I agree that such analyses would make this study more accurate and more complete, I would also never have finished it. I am neither mathematician nor scientist, and must leave it to others to fill in the gaps in my work. In fact, one of my purposes is to challenge Peirce scholars to do exactly that.

Others may wish for more discussion of Peirce's many remarks—usually derogatory—about churches and theologians. While these matters are interesting, they belong to the philosophy of religion, as distinguished from what is usually today called "philosophical theology." Peirce himself would not have used this expression, but since it is the contemporary name for inquiry into the being and nature of a deity, I use "philosophical theology" to designate the area of theorizing into which this study now falls.

Another expression I use continually is "conception." I choose this in preference to concept, notion, or idea, because Peirce himself used it repeatedly in the pragmatic maxim (CP 5.402). By a "conception," Peirce explained, he meant "the rational purport of a word or other expression [which] lies exclusively in its conceivable bearing upon the conduct of life." (CP 5.412) My own frequent use of this word attempts to capture and express Peirce's own pragmatic intent in *his* uses of the word.

These matters, as well as the whole question of religious language in general, lie within the territory Peirce called the "ethics of terminology." Authors, he often argued, have a moral obligation to use words in the sense which their original authors gave to them so that philosophical vocabulary may soon come to resemble the technical nomenclature of the sciences (CP 5.413; Ketner, 1981). The breakdown of this attempt in the case of religious language, language which is older than any of its users and peculiarly resistant to the formulation of precise technical definition, created the necessity for a theory of the intrinsic vagueness of religious —and some other—language, a topic for a later chapter. But even in the cases of "God," "theism," and "deity," Peirce attempted, as we shall see, to retain a connection with the senses in which these terms are ordinarily used, even though he stretched them considerably.

This study is largely a work of assemblage. In order to show what Peirce thought about deity at each stage of his career, and to show that at each period he was refining his philosophical theology in dialogue with whatever else he was learning, I have collected from his writings much of his commentary on theological topics. Because much of this material is scattered in the manuscripts and not yet widely available, and in an effort to let Peirce speak for himself, I have quoted a good deal. Within these quotations, the reader can assume that the italics are Peirce's unless otherwise noted. I have also, within quotations, retained his spelling. Thankfully, I could not have eliminated his humor if I had wanted to do so.

Several persons have helped me significantly with this study. Vincent Potter mentored the dissertation of which this forms a revision. Andrine Baker, Molly Hite, Kenneth Ketner, and Joseph Ransdell have all read and criticized the text, although I have used only some of their suggestions and the mistakes remain mine. Quentin Lauer not only read the dissertation but also discussed with me for years the questions addressed here. Kenneth Ketner gave me many other helpful suggestions, including gentle ones to get the job done. The philosophy department of Harvard University has graciously given permission to publish materials from Peirce's manuscripts in Houghton Library. To all of these people I am thankful and above all to Max Fisch, whose willingness to share his time and resources makes Peirce's "community of inquirers" real for me.

Chapter I

THE PRE-1867 WRITINGS

Religious questions fascinated Charles Sanders Peirce from his college years onward. As he developed his theory of categories—which culminated in "On a New List of Categories" in 1866—and his early semiotic of the 1866 Lowell Lectures, he continually asked questions about the nature of God or of the infinite, and about the cognitive status of any religious conceptions. In this chapter I will note some biographical data and early intellectual influences, as well as study several early manuscripts, in an effort to characterize Peirce's early religious views.

EARLY INFLUENCES

Before Peirce read any philosophy at all, he grew up in a Unitarian home where religion was taken seriously and science seen as the study of God's works (Murphey, 1961: 13-16), but where dogma and religious differences were taken lightly. When, after graduation from college and before his first marriage, he joined the Episcopalian church, of which he remained a member until his death, his father and other family members welcomed this development. His Unitarian background makes it not at all surprising that throughout his life, Peirce should have exhibited an intense dislike of dogmatism and intolerance in religion, together with a strong disposition to believe "the general essence and spirit of it." (MS L408: 25 July 1907) His early writings show little direct influence of Unitarianism. Since he was already deeply into the study of Kant, and by 1862 had joined the Trinitarian Episcopalians, this is not surprising.

Another early influence, Peirce's exposure to Concord Transcendentalism, probably also antedates his reading of philosophy. He later remembered that Emerson and Margaret Fuller had been guests in the family home (SS 113-14). His earliest list of his books, compiled 8 February 1858, includes various works of Emerson (MS 1555).

In the 1890s Peirce would give apparently inconsistent accounts of his relation to the Transcendentalists. The 1892 "Law of Mind" suggests that any influence was remote, not immediate:

> ... I was born and reared in the neighborhood of Concord—I mean in Cambridge—at the time when Emerson, Hedge, and their friends were disseminating the ideas that they had caught from Schelling, and Schelling from Plotinus, from Boehme, or from God knows what minds stricken with the monstrous mysticism of the East. But the atmosphere of Cambridge held many an antisceptic against Concord transcendentalism; and I am not conscious of having contracted any of that virus. Nevertheless, it is probable that some cultured bacilli, some benignant form of the disease was implanted in my soul, unawares, and that now, after long incubation, it comes to the surface, modified by mathematical conceptions and by training in physical investigations. (CP 6.102)

Still, in that same year of 1892, he admitted a stronger connection. In a draft of a response to Paul Carus's characterization of him as a modern Hume, he declared, "The truth is I am a sort of Schellingian, or New England Transcendentalist; and the man who thinks he can refute me with arguments intended for Hume, may have reason to call himself a logical 'butterfingers'." (MS 958) In another draft he could "frankly pigeonhole myself as a modified Schellingian, or New England transcendentalist." (MS 958) These ironic statements, however, need to be read in context, keeping in mind the contrast he wanted to draw between his own beliefs and attitudes and those of Hume. Taken alone these remarks tell us nothing about Peirce's views in his early years when he was actually being exposed to the Transcendentalists. He had, however, characterized himself in 1859: "List of Horrid Things I am: Realist, Materialist, Transcendentalist, Idealist." (MS 921)

The difficulty with identifying transcendentalism of an Emersonian kind in Peirce's early writings is that he was also studying Kant at this time. The early manuscripts often use the expressions "transcendental" and "transcendentalist" in clear reference to Kant's philosophy. Thus, for example, in 1864-1865, "Other opinions besides those of Hume, Reid, and Kant are still extant; but these are the most widely influential. They are the philosophies of positivism, common-sense, and transcendentalism." (MS 349) Peirce may, at least for a time, have regarded Kant as the legitimate forerunner of the Concord Transcendentalists. In his 1862 "Notes for a Work on Metaphysics" we find this:

> I shall now show 1st that the Transcendentalists conclude with a return to faith, 2nd that the use they make of it is the source of all that is valuable in their investigations, and 3rd that while their own faith is necessarily blind, their reasoning is not so close as to leave no room for

faith demonstrating trustworthiness. I will first review the researches of Kant . . . .(MS 922)

It is not clear just who the Transcendentalists referred to in this passage were. Kant may be one, or may just be an ancestor. Neither Schelling nor Hegel had appeared in Peirce's library even by 1866. As evidence for any very early influence of the Concord variety, we have only Peirce's later recollection that prominent Transcendentalists had been in his home, and his confession in the "list of horrid things" that he was a transcendentalist.

If, however, he did take an interest in them at this time, and in their relation to Kant, the reason must have been the faith-reason problem, the question of whether knowledge of God is really knowledge. Like Coleridge, the Concord Transcendentalists distinguished between Understanding, the faculty of scientific knowing, and Reason, which gives intuitive knowledge of God in Nature. Like Kant, they could be said to restrict the realm of knowledge in order to make room for faith. At least for a short time in early 1859, Peirce may have toyed with the view of both Kant and the Transcendentalists that faith functioned outside the cognitive domain. In his notes on Henry Longueville Mansel (see below) we find:

1. Human reason is impotent as an *a priori* judge of truth concerning God or is impotent in Theology. 2. Reasoning should not disturb either a Theist's or Atheist's belief. (MS 921)

Temporary acceptance of this view may be, in fact, exactly what he meant by calling himself a transcendentalist in this same manuscript. Furthermore, the young Peirce would surely have been aware of the Transcendentalist's vaguely pantheistic view of God's nature, though the Trinitarianism of the Episcopalians affected his thought more deeply, as we shall see.

If we don't know that Peirce was explicitly aware of Concord Transcendentalist doctrine before he began to read Kant, we do know that he had read one philosophical book which may have inclined him to be receptive to both varieties of "transcendentalism." Peirce later recalled that his work in philosophy had begun with the study of the poet Friedrich Schiller's *Aesthetische Briefe,* "a very good book for an infant philosopher." (MS 310: 1903) In 1906 he listed Schiller as one of five authors who had helped to form his thought on the question of ultimate purpose (CP 5.402n).

A glance at the poet Schiller's work shows many places where an "infant philosopher"—not to mention the C. S. Peirce who looked back in the early 1900s—may have found suggestions about the importance and the religious character of an esthetic ideal. "Those who do not venture out beyond actuality," Schiller says, "will never capture Truth." (1954: 50) Beauty, esthetic ideals, and feeling—not mere facts—are needed for moral education. In addition, Schiller's insistence that feeling and reason are separate realms of human experience (1954: 68n) may have inclined the young Peirce toward his lifelong belief in a role for instinct and sentiment in moral and religious matters. *Aesthetische Briefe* also contains an emphasis on the role of play and the "play-impulse" in the search for truth (SS 77).

It is not surprising, then, to find Peirce in his early twenties writing what sound like early versions of the 1908 "Humble Argument." On 1 April 1860, for example, in a notebook entitled "Private thoughts principally on the conducted life," Peirce described solitude as "drawing nigh unto the personality in nature, and that it is, in a humble sense, walking with God . . . ." (MS 921)

Even more striking is this passage from his 1863 Cambridge High School reunion lecture entitled "The Place of Our Age in the History of Civilization":

> A man looks upon nature, sees its sublimity and beauty, and his spirit gradually rises to the idea of a God. He does not see the divinity, nor does nature prove to him the existence of that Being, but it does excite his mind and his imagination until the idea becomes rooted in his heart . . . . (Weiner, 1958: 10; cf. CP 6.458-461 and 6.467)

It is true that these two passages contain no reference to Schiller's play-impulse, but if they were taken together with it, the resemblance to the 1908 "Neglected Argument for the Reality of God" (CP 6.452-491) would be quite close. Such a resemblance supports my view that Peirce's very late attention to religion was indeed continuous with his youthful beliefs and concerns.

Finally, a word about the conceptions of God embodied in the *Aesthetische Briefe*. Schiller uses the term "God" only once, in reference to the degrading, fearful spirit in which some people worship (1954: 118). He speaks more often of the Absolute, of the Infinite, expressions which also appear as references to God in Peirce's early writings. Schiller will say, for example, "The pure moral impulse is directed at the Absolute..." (1954: 53) or will speak of a "representation of the Infinite." (1954: 73) It would be rash to conclude that Peirce derived even his earliest uses of these terms from Schiller alone, but we do know that Peirce read this book, and that he later considered it to have been an important influence in the early development of his thought.

Kant and Mansel

Since Schiller's own favorite philosopher was Kant, Peirce's step into Kant's *Critique of Pure Reason* must have seemed a natural one. Peirce had entered Harvard in 1855, and soon began the two years in which, by his own account, he read the first Critique for two hours a day, until he almost had it by heart (SS 114). In 1898 he remembered that:

> In the early sixties I was a passionate devotee of Kant, at least as regarded the Transcendental Analytic in the Critic of the Pure Reason. I believed more implicitly in the two tables of the Functions of Judgment and the Categories than if they had been brought down from Sinai. (CP 4.2)

A look at the manuscript brings more precision to Peirce's memory here. Already in the fifties and certainly by 1860, he seemed to be trying to work out his own categories (Buzzelli, 1974: 7). More importantly, as hinted even in the passage quoted above, Peirce entertained doubts about the noumenon very early. "Wherever there is knowledge there is faith. Wherever there is faith (properly speaking, that is) knowledge." (MS 920) Thus Peirce rejected the faith-reason dichotomy, as well as the view that there are objects of faith which are not and cannot be objects of knowledge. Even the titles of early essays, for example, "Why We Can Reason on the Infinite," indicate dissatisfaction with Kant's solutions. Even so he continued to consider Kant a great logician—after all, Peirce thought, only Kant and Aristotle had realized that logic was the key to philosophy. Peirce used Kant as his principal reference point and dialogue partner throughout this period, at least until about 1866 when his study of the medieval scholastics began to exert a strong influence on his writings.

Several manuscripts from the years 1857-1862 show the effects of Peirce's struggles with Kant's categories upon his early speculations in what we would call philosophical theology. I will examine these writings from two angles: (1) the use of the expression "Influx" in the "The Modus of the It" and in other writings from this period; and (2) Peirce's 1859 attempts to understand and refute Henry Longueville Mansel's extreme faith-reason dichotomy.

Among the cryptic expressions to be found in these early manuscripts is the term "Influx." It was being used at that time in a variety of senses, most of which had something to do with a flow of some kind of spiritual influence into a mind or body. George Ellis and Peirce's teacher, Frederic Dan Huntington, were using the term in their religious revival to distinguish their views from the dominant Unitarian ethic of self-development. Human religion, they taught, depends on divine gift (Smith, 1957: 97-102). "Influx" in their usage suggests the theological doctrine of grace. The Swedenborgians, on the other hand, seem to have used the term very loosely as a link in their doctrine of correspondences, for example, between mental and physical phenomena (Swedenborg 1976: #88, #340).

Peirce must have been aware of these usages and seems to have created some of his own (Buzzelli, 1974: 36n60). The term first appears in an 1857 manuscript entitled "The Modus of the It" (MS 916). Among the necessary modes, Peirce distinguished "that whose necessity is [an] absolute, and self-dependent of existence of a quality, influx." But, he continued,

> ... there are three kinds of influxual derivation. 1. that whose influx is of possible mode or negation; 2. that whose influx is of actual mode or reality; and 3 that whose influx is of necessary mode (the modes of possibility and actuality being coextensive) or infinity.
>
> Of these only reality is anything to us. Why was the influx actual and the derivation more than negation? Because into the negation was worked infinite quality which since in all that was possible was actual[ly] lured the negation to a reality. (MS 916)

Perhaps an early creation-cosmology can be read here. For mere possibility to become actual, the activity of the infinite and necessary is required. The infinite lures the possible into reality. The necessary mode of influx creates the real world. These three modes of influxual derivation also show how early the categorial triad—his later Firstness, Secondness, and Thirdness—began to take form for Peirce.

Two years later, remarking on the difficulty which the conception of the Perfect causes to metaphysics, he enumerated without elaboration, four kinds of perfection: totality, infinity, influx and necessity (MS 921: 24 May 1859). He did not say four qualities of the perfect, but four kinds of perfection. Perhaps he intended to say that the deity possesses these four kinds of perfection. Or he may have meant that the ideal of perfection can take any or all of these forms.

Another fragment from this period (MS 858) suggests that influx is the impression that any object makes on a knower: "That which may be thought of, which is a source of influx I call a thing." (MS 858) Perhaps influx is simply a relation of influence between any two things. The influenced thing—in this case the thought—depends upon the source of influence—in this case, the thing.

But "influx" does seem to have more special senses in these early writings. As noted above influx is one kind of perfection, and "perfection" is a term Peirce often used in this period, and sometimes later, to refer to God. We find, for example, a paper entitled "Influx: Proof of the Infinite Nature of the Creator":

> The necessary sequence of cause and effect is inseparable from time, therefore, this began when time began, and therefore time also was *created* when the Universe was created. Therefore this whole sequence of Causation in time has the dependence of Creation, which is Influx. Therefore since the Universe has been a-going from everlasting the amount of Spiritual Manifestation is Infinite. (MS 859)

Apparently the Creator, the Spiritual Manifestation, the Influx, the Creation, and causation are all infinite; and each of these terms involves all the others. Depending on how the "which" in the second sentence is taken, "Influx" could be equivalent to Creation, to the dependence of Creation, or to the whole sequence of Causation in time, or to all three. perhaps Influx is spiritual manifestation, spiritual manifestation is creation and the creator whose nature and spiritual manifestation are infinite is God.

Finally, in MS 921 we find this undated fragment:

> ... the Reason is at one in substance with all things. It, in common with the Pan, stands in dependence of Influx on God. They all emanate from him. Reasonableness therefore signifies being of the Whole, which is simply Existence.

Possibly the young Peirce held an emanationist view of Creation, and at least part of his conception of God would have been a conception of the source of emanation. Influx may, among other things, be the process of emanation itself. Again,

> Not only the perfect degrees of modality, but all degree whatsoever has one of three successive stages. The first is nullity, the second positivity, and the third Perfection. I call these successive and not retrogressive because they are stages toward perfection.
>
> Not only the successive stages of degree but all stage whatever has one of these three temporal expressions . . . . (MS 858)

Influx then, in Peirce's early vocabulary—it does not, to my knowledge, appear in his later writings—has both a general sense of dependency of any effect on a cause, and a special sense of something like divine creativity. This creative process can be seen either as God's self-expression, or as creation's dependence on God, or both.

More obviously related to Peirce's studies of Kant is his dialogue with Henry Longueville Mansel, an English apologist and follower of both Kant and Hamilton on the question of the limits of reason and the necessity of faith. Mansel's *The Limits of Religious Thought* appeared in 1858, and attracted much attention in both England and America. Peirce listed this book, together with Mansel's earlier *Metaphysics*, among his books in 1866 (MS 1556). Mansel's favorite terms for God, considered as an object of thought, were "First Cause," and "the Absolute and Infinite." Mansel presented Kantian-sounding arguments for regarding reason as useless and contradictory in the area of religion, and concluded that it is not possible to argue consistently for or against theism. He also believed that any God of reason had to be a pantheistic conception—the mere sum of all reality. His apologetic, then, like that of Kierkegaard, was based on the absolute necessity of faith.

The term "Absolute" meant to Mansel "that which exists in itself, having no necessary relation to any other Being" (Mansel, 1859: 45); by "Infinite" he meant "that which is free from all possible limitations; that than which a greater is inconceivable; and which consequently can receive no additional attribute or mode of existence which it had not from all eternity." (1859: 45) Taken together, "the absolute and infinite must necessarily, as the profoundest metaphysicians have acknowledged, amount to nothing less than the sum of all reality." (1859: 46)

According to Mansel, the pantheistic conception contradicts the idea of God as first cause, and the "Absolute and Infinite" is itself a conception riddled with internal contradictions. It "cannot be conceived as the sum of all existence; nor yet can it be conceived as a part only of that sum." (1859: 58-59) Mansel concluded that reason is useless as a means of reaching or refuting religious belief. The object of religious faith is simply not within the competence of reasoning.

Two early Peirce manuscripts contain extensive notes on Mansel's book. MS S66 is a detailed outline of Mansel's basic argument; MS 921 contains, with page numbers, quotations and paraphrases from the Boston 1859 edition of *The Limits of Religious Thought*. Peirce's paraphrase of Mansel's conclusion took this form:

> Human reason is impotent as an *a priori* judge of truth concerning God, or is impotent in theology.
> Reasoning should not disturb either a Theist's or an Atheist's belief. (MS 921)

Neither of these manuscripts provides any evidence that Peirce accepted or rejected Mansel's views, only that he studied them carefully.

But MS 858 (1859), "An Essay on the Limits of Religious Thought written to prove that we can reason upon the nature of God," whose title surely alludes to that of Mansel's book does show that Peirce almost immediately rejected Mansel's exclusion of reason from the house of religion. He began by asserting that we can reason about anything we can define, whether or not such a thing exists in imagination or in nature. Many things which we can never comprehend can be given intelligible definitions:

> I will give two instances of this; one simple and the other practical. Suppose somebody should talk about an OG/X and when you ask him what he meant he should say it was a four-sided triangle. You would proceed to show that he had no such conception[,] that nobody had. You would reason upon that which you could not conceive of. This instance is too elementary. Suppose someone should tell me he could imagine two persons interchanging identities. I should proceed to reason on the pretended imagination and show that it was inconceivable.
> We can therefore comprehend definitions, when we cannot conceive of that which they define . . . . (MS 858)

Peirce then proposed to explain how the infinite might be defined, if not conceived, as a simple idea resulting from the intersection of "complex and crossing relations." Next he listed a series of triadic categories from which might emerge a definition of the infinite: the three necessary modes of dependency as community, causality, and influx; the perfect degrees of modality as possibility, actuality, and necessity; three stages of all degrees as nullity, positivity, and perfection; three temporal expressions of each stage as retrogression, contemporaneity, and succession; formal intuitions of expression as consciousness, space, and time; total quantities of intuition as notion, substance, and form; infinite—"because possessed beyond limitation"—qualities of quantity; unity, plurality, totality; and finally, three influxual dependencies of quality as negation, reality, and infinity (MS 858).

So Peirce, with his Kantian-sounding system of categories, diverged from Kant in locating God or infinity within the categorial system. Furthermore, if Buzzelli (1974: 7) is right in saying that Peirce shifted early to a material conception of the categories, then infinity—or the nature of God—can be an object of thought, and faith need not be unreasonable. Indeed, Peirce apparently had exactly this point in mind: "I have run through the categories in this way in order to show precisely what infinity is and where in the scheme of conceptions it stands." (MS 858) Since infinity is a source of influx, and can be thought of, it is a thing. (MS 858) In other words, as a variant within the same manuscript explains, the theory is realistic even if infinity is not exactly a thing or a quality.

The variant also explains what Peirce meant by infinity as "influxual dependency of quality":

> What is infinity? It is not the conception of a thing, neither is it the conception of the quality of a thing. If we can think of a good man, it is because in the first place we have a notion of man and in the second place we have the conception of good and in the third place we can combine one conception with the other. When this is done, I express the synthesis by saying that an influxual dependence of *good* upon *man* is conceived of. Influxual dependence has three degrees. 1st it may be negative as when we say *the man is not good.* 2nd it may be real as when we say *the man is more or less good* or *pretty good* or *very good,* in short when he has goodness in degree, and 3rd it is infinite when we say *he is perfectly good.* Then he has goodness beyond degree. Infinity then is only to be predicated of qualities and only of qualities conceived to be possessed. We can therefore analyse the conception of infinity[,] we can state its relations to other conceptions although the conception itself we never have. (MS 858)

Thus although Peirce was not sure whether God was a thing or some kind of qualitative perfection-relation, the importance of this essay lies in the rejection of the Kant-Hamilton-Mansel view that the question of the nature of God is outside the competence of reason and must be left to faith. On the contrary, faith and reason may agree about the infinite:

> When a thing influences the soul its effect comes into the field of consciousness or not. In the former case we call its influence an unconscious idea. Now *Faith* says, the infinite does influence the soul—as infinite. It follows that we have an unconscious idea of it. This is where the infinite belongs. (MS 858)

"Unconscious" here must not be taken in a Freudian sense, but rather probably as "not fully definite," but nonetheless real and efficacious. In later years Peirce would hold the idea of God, though not of the infinite, to be intrinsically vague but full of pragmatic import and therefore cognizable. Even in 1862 he thought both faith and reason necessary in all thought. On 30 March 1862, for example, he wrote: "Faith is not peculiar to or more needed in one province of thought than in another. For every premiss we require faith and nowhere else is there any room for it. This is overlooked by Kant and others who draw a distinction between knowledge and faith. Wherever there is faith (properly speaking, that is) knowledge." (MS 920; similar passages in MS 922 dated 29 May 1862)

Peirce's 1862 adoption of "realistic pantheism" closes this period of his dialogue with Mansel, whose fear of pantheism had formed part of the basis for his single-minded reliance on revelation and faith. When Peirce claimed, in these early manuscripts, to be able to reason about the infinite, and that therefore the infinite is in some way part of the categorial system, he was also claiming to be able to reason about God. He did, however, accept Kant's view of reasoning as the imposition of some kind of unity on a sensory manifold. Thus reasoning about the Infinite may be equivalent to reasoning about all phenomena. On 25 July 1859 he wrote:

> The noumenon tree we can never know. The phenomenon of God we can always apprehend. If this simple distinction be kept in view, where is the puzzle, where is the contradiction of the infinite and absolute? (MS 921)

Thus it was Peirce's rejection of a world in itself which reasoning cannot reach that led him to include "the Infinite" within the universe governed by the categories, or even at times to make the infinite itself a category. This period, then, saw Peirce move from his Kant-worship of the fifties to his assertion of the knowability of God, from which in turn he developed his conception of God. Detailed analysis of Peirce's work on Kant's categories and on his own is beyond the scope of this study, but it is because the three categories covered all that can be known that Peirce came to assert the cognizability of the Infinite.

Not surprisingly then, as he worked on the logic of Kant's categories, Peirce called his metaphysical position "Realistic Pantheism," and described it thus in identical sections of MSS 920 and 922:

> Realistic Pantheism: From Idealism, it follows that nothing exists which is not of-thinkable as thought. From Materialism, it follows that nothing but the unthought exists. That which being unthinkable is of-thinkable as thought is Perfection, In Chapter III of the Introduction it was shown that Perfection is God. Hence, nothing exists but God.
>
> Here then we have three worlds Matter Mind God mutually excluding and including each other, as I showed was possible . . . .

Peirce had concluded that not only do these three worlds include each other, but also that they require each other. They are not merely different ways of speaking of whatever is, but indeed are realities themselves: (1) the ideal reality of what is real only as thought, (2) the material reality of the unthought (even the "nothing but" the unthought), and (3) the reality of Perfection, the thought of the unthinkable.

Peirce's account of "realistic pantheism" contains an interesting feature: that the three worlds not only mutually include one another, but also exclude one another. Each of the three worlds is both immanent and transcendent with respect to the other two—a peculiar sort of pantheism.

A final cryptic expression Peirce employed in this period is "the Perfect" or "Perfection" to replace "God." (MS 920; 922) It is difficult to tell from the contexts what Peirce meant by these expressions, but he did say that perfection comes in four varieties: totality, infinity, influx, and necessity. These last three—if influx is taken to mean creativity of some type—sound like traditional descriptions of God. Totality may be completion, that outside which there is nothing. But what is perfection itself? Later Peirce would define it as "the state or degree of completeness, excellency that leaves nothing to be desired," and absolute perfection as "the absence of every kind of defect and fault, the perfection of God." Essential or transcendental perfection he would define as "the possession of everything that is necessary to an essence." (MS 1166) It is dangerous to read these definitions back into the early papers, but perhaps Peirce was groping for a conception of God as the all, the completely whole, or the self-sufficient. "Nothing has a self-dependent existence but the divinity." (MS 920; 30 March 1862)

In summary, then, the importance of this period of wrestling with Kant and Mansel over the faith-reason question lies in its implications for the question of the nature of a deity. If it be admitted that God cannot be known but only accepted on faith, then there is no reasonable way to say that one conception of God is better than another. The upshot of the Kantian view as carried to Mansel's extremes is usually biblical fundamentalism, as

Mansel's own case shows. On the other hand, if reason is once admitted into the realm of religion, the fear arises that God may be reduced to human proportions, and faith may have no place. In addition, the effort to make the idea of God precise may lead to the dogmatism and creedal divisions Peirce later so often deplored. As he emerged from his earliest Kantian period in 1861 and 1862, he tried to make room for faith as an essential part of the knowing process, and thus to overcome the problems which result from restricting religion either to faith or to rational theologies.

More Early Influences

Meanwhile, in 1859, Darwin's *Origin of Species* had appeared. Although Peirce did not write anything in support of evolutionary theories until the mid-1880s (Fisch 1971: 194-5), he must have followed closely the controversy which ensued upon the appearance of this world-shaking book. Louis Agassiz, who held for the creation of fixed species, was one of Benjamin Peirce's closest friends, though the elder Peirce seems to have kept an open mind toward evolutionary theories (Murphey 1961: 13-14). Charles Peirce had studied in college with Asa Gray, who believed religion and evolutionary theories were not necessarily opposed. Later Peirce studied classification with Agassiz, and admitted having been influenced by him (CP 1.205n; 1.229-31). Also, if his memory is to be trusted, he was in contact with Chauncey Wright from at least 1860 (CP 5.64). Wright was a Darwin enthusiast and though Peirce told him the "ideas of development had more vitality by far than any of his other favorite conceptions" (CP 5.64), there is no evidence in Peirce's writings in the early and middle sixties of the influence of "Darwin's great work."

In 1862, apparently under the influence of his future wife, Harriet Melusina Fay, Peirce joined the Episcopal Church, of which he remained a lifelong member, and to which he returned as a communicant from 1892 forward (MS L483). His post-confirmation writings, the Cambridge High School Association lecture and his lecture on positivism, for example, show increased concern for the roles of religion and churches in life and civilization, but it is not evident that his Episcopalian confirmation produced any immediate effect on his conception of God. One result, however, might be the interest in Trinitarian conceptions which appears in Lecture XI of the 1866 Lowell Lectures, but this could also be due to his study of the medieval scholastics.

Peirce began in the middle to late 1860s an intensive reading of Aristotle and the medieval scholastics (Fisch 1967: 165). These readings, especially in Scotus and Aquinas, were mainly devoted to logical problems and to finding the resources to work out his difficulties with Kant. From 1865 on, his writings contain an abundance of scholastic terminology, and by the time this early period ends with "On a New List of Categories" in 1867, and the *Journal of Speculative Philosophy* articles of 1868, a heavy scholastic influence is apparent in his thought. Since Peirce was a careful reader, even though his main interest in these thinkers was in logic, it cannot have escaped him that *their* main interest was in theological problems. Nor can he have failed to gain a familiarity with their formulations of these problems and with their methods of approaching them. His writings after this reading period do in fact indicate such familiarity, but show no propensity to adopt their solutions in any explicit way (Boler, 1963).

Because the relationship of Henry James Sr., Swedenborg, and Peirce has already been well discussed elsewhere (Krolikowski, 1964; Trammell, 1973), I will make only a few remarks here. As early as 1864-1865 Peirce mentioned Swedenborg in logic examples (MS 343). He may have been reading him before the James family moved to Boston in 1866 when he began to spend time conversing with Henry James the father. This influence—and such Peirce himself accounted it (CP 5.402n)—of James and of Swedenborg himself, showed itself more strongly in the Arisbe period. In these early years, however, James's interest in Hegel may have led Peirce to read Hegel (James, 1914: 287-89). In addition, James liked to distinguish between existence and being (James, 1914: 287-89). It is true that Peirce was doing this before the James family came to Boston, but James's *Substance and Shadow* was published in Boston in 1863, and is listed among Peirce's books in 1866.

Cambridge High School Lecture of 1863

Not long after he began his study of the scholastics, Peirce, now aged 24, delivered a lecture at the reunion of the Cambridge High School Association on 12 November 1863, a lecture he entitled "The Place of Our Age in the History of Civilization," and later described as a "Hegel-like paper" (MS 958). Toward the beginning he imagined Dante watching the human mind do its creative and critical work in the seventeenth, eighteenth, and nineteenth centuries, and concluded that "he who viewed Hell without dismay would fall to the earth quailing before the terrific might of intellect that God has scattered broadcast over this whole age." (Wiener, 1958: 5) This God acts in such a way as to spread intellect around—even intellect which criticizes religion—an interesting idea in view of Peirce's later tendency to suggest a near identification between God and the growth of reasonableness.

Peirce then went on to distinguish "our age" from that of the Reformation, and to give a brief history of modern philosophy, emphasizing its sceptical character. He concluded this section with the following comments on Kant and Hegel:

> ... Kant presented a more insoluble doubt than all the rest, and one which has not been answered to this day, for while he showed that our innate ideas of space, time, quantity, reality, cause, possibility, and so on are true, he found himself utterly unable to do this respecting the ideas of Immortality, Freedom, and God. Accordingly, all

metaphysicians since his time have been endeavoring to remove this difficulty, but not altogether with success.

Hegel's system seemed, at first, satisfactory, but its further development resulted in Strauss' *Life of Jesus,* against which the human soul, the datum upon which he proceeded, itself cried out; the sense of mankind, which he had elevated into a God, itself repudiated the claim. We thus see, however, that all the progress we have made in philosophy, that is, all that has been made since the Greeks, is the result of that methodological scepticism which is the first element of human freedom. (Wiener, 1958: 8)

This passage indicates, first of all, that Peirce was not as of this date satisfied with any of the solutions, including his own trials, to Kant's "insoluble doubt." Neither the inclusion of God within the realm of the Categories (realistic pantheism) nor the exclusion creating the two domains of faith and reason (Mansel's answer) left him comfortable. He had not yet discovered, to his own satisfaction, either the nature or the knowability of "God, freedom, and immortality." Nor did Peirce specify to whom Hegel's system at first seemed satisfactory. Apparently he had not himself read Hegel at this time, though he had read Augusto Vera's *Introduction à la philosophie de Hegel* (see MS 1555). Peirce's criticism was that the "sense of mankind" refuses to be elevated into identification with God. We are aware of ourselves as less than divine. Clearly Peirce found what he took to be Hegel's solution to Kant's problem unsatisfying. God is somehow more than "the sense of mankind."

Peirce concluded this passage in favor of "methodological scepticism." His later castigation of Descartes' "paper doubt" (CP 5.265; 6.498) makes his later "fallibilism," that is, a disposition to regard all scientific and philosophical conclusions as corrigible. If any progress is to be made in solving Kant's problem about God, Freedom, and Immortality, he seemed to be saying, inquiry—not dogmatism—is the route to take.

The lecture goes on to discuss the function of Christianity in the growth of civilization. According to Peirce, Christians must believe "that Christ is now directing the course of history and presiding over the destinies of kings, and that there is no branch of the public weal which does not come within the bounds of his realm." (Wiener, 1958: 9) At this point, soon after his confirmation in the Episcopal Church, Peirce apparently accepted the divinity of Jesus, and saw this divinity as consisting in governance of the universe.

A section of this lecture describes a process by which the idea of God arises in human beings:

Religion ought not to be regarded either as a subjective or an objective phenomenon. That is to say, it is neither something within us nor yet altogether without us—but bears a third relation to us, namely, that of existing in our communion with another being. Nevertheless, religion may be revealed in either of three ways—by an inward self-development, or by seeing it about us, or by a personal communication from the Most High. An example of revealed religion in the first way is natural religion. A man looks upon nature, sees its sublimity and beauty, and his spirit gradually rises to the idea of a God. He does not see the Divinity, nor does nature prove to him the existence of that Being, but it does excite his mind and his imagination until the idea becomes rooted in his heart. In the same way, the continual change and movement in nature suggest the idea of omnipresence. And finally, by the events in his own life, he becomes persuaded of the relation of that Being with his own soul. Such a religion, where all is hinted, nought revealed, is natural religion. (Wiener, 1958: 10)

In this extract, Peirce used several names and descriptions for the deity. "Another being"—neither wholly within nor wholly without—reinforces the impression that Peirce was carefully trying to maintain an immanence-transcendence balance. "Most High" seems to indicate basic acceptance of a biblical God who acts through historical events but is not wholly identified with them. "The Divinity" is a rather neutral term, favored by Unitarians, without particular religious or philosophical implications. "Omnipresence" suggests immanence, but in the context leaves open the possibility that to be present is to be other than that in which or to which one is present. (That change and movement suggests divine omnipresence to the young Peirce may mark a point of continuity with his later opinion that growth is an indicator of God's reality). Finally, a "Being" related with one's own soul may be immanent, but must be other than that to which it is related, as Peirce had pointed out in his statement on Strauss and Hegel.

Aside from the clues found in an inspection of terminology, and from the resemblance of this passage to the 1908 "humble argument" (CP 6.452-491), two other points stand out. First, existence is not important here. Peirce did not claim that nature proves the existence of God, and thus did not have to argue against Hume. The idea of a being, not its existence, is in question here, and the idea is suggested rather than strictly proven. *Things* exist, and Peirce apparently already leaned toward rejecting the notion of God as a thing among other things.

A second important aspect of the nature of the deity seems to be the capacity for relatedness and for communion with human beings. If this is true, God must have something in common with human persons to serve as the basis for relationship. God must also be other than those beings to whom God is related, or with whom God is in communion. This relational character of God may also form a foundation for the personal character of God on which Peirce later insisted (CP 6.157; 6.435).

Further on, after an examination of idealism and materialism which concluded that they require each other, Peirce approvingly attributed to

Bacon the view that the *end* of science is the glory of God. Here Benjamin Peirce's son may be heard to appropriate his father's conviction that science is the study of God's works, and that God is to be found within the world into which science inquires.

The final paragraph of this address could have been written by an Emerson:

> When the conclusion of our age comes, and scepticism and materialism have done their perfect work, we shall have a far greater faith than ever before. For then man will see God's wisdom and mercy, not only in every event of his own life, but in that of the gorilla, the lion, the fish, the polyp, the tree, the crystal, the grain of dust, the atom. He will see that each one of these has an inward existence of its own, for which God loves it, and that he has given to it a nature of endless perfectibility. He will see the folly of saying that nature was created for his use. He will see that God has no other creation than his children. So the poet in our days—and the true poet is the true prophet—personifies everything, not rhetorically but in his own feelings. He tells us that he feels an affinity for nature, and loves the stone or the drops of water. But the time is coming when there shall be no more poetry, for that which was poetically divined shall be scientifically known. . . . Philosophy will have taught us that it is this *all* which constitutes the church. (Wiener, 1958: 13)

Peirce looked forward to a time when the attributes of a personal God, wisdom and mercy, would be seen in the personality of all natural things. What the poet divines, science and philosophy will know. Perhaps the "poetically divined" becomes the abductive hypothesis for Peirce, and when the rest of the process of inquiry is complete in the long run, we will scientifically and philosophically know the holiness or divinity of the "all." Perhaps Peirce was not in possession of his fully developed logic of inquiry in 1863, but its genesis may have been there. Speculations on the nature of God may even have provided some of the impetus toward the development of such a logic.

Sometime before 1866 (Fisch, 1974: 174-6; 189), Peirce began to read Hegel. MS 340 lists a planned but apparently undelivered lecture on Hegel's logic for Peirce's Harvard series "On the Logic of Science" for the spring of 1865. In Lecture VII of this same series, Peirce remarked that

> . . . perhaps the strongest point of Hegelianism is the purely impersonal character which it attributes to the unity of apperception. In this respect, I follow Hegel; but I do so without budging from the critical standpoint. (MS 346)

In other words, Hegel freed logic from psychology—for that much, at least, Peirce could admire him. In fact, he would later write:

> My three categories . . . resulted from two years incessant study in the direction of trying to do what Hegel tried to do. It became apparent that there were such categories as his. But bad as his are, I could substitute nothing radically better. (MS 1338)

So, at least in terms of categories, it seems fair to say that the years 1856-1867 saw Peirce move from Kant to Hegel. It may be that this same movement can be detected in regard to the nature and knowledge of God. Kant had restricted God to the noumenal sphere which can be apprehended only by faith. Peirce, on the contrary, early saw faith involved in all inquiry—all cognition as inference. Insisting that whatever is can be known, he brought the noumena back into the realm governed by categories, and thus labeled himself a transcendentalist. By the end of this period Peirce was sure that there are no incognizable things-in-themselves. But much more evidence of Peirce's dialogue with Hegel does not appear again until the 1890s.

POSITIVISM AND THE LOGIC OF SCIENCE

Peirce's critique of positivism (MS 970: 1867-1868) is fascinating from several points of view: it shows his clear difference with positivists of both nineteenth and twentieth century varieties; its emphasis on the consequences of ideas and theories reads like a preview of the pragmatism of the late 1870s; its concern with the nominalism-realism question presages the review of Berkeley in 1870; it treats the logic of hypothesis and of theory; and it would be a rich mine for the study of Peirce's early philosophy of religion. For the moment, however, I shall focus upon Peirce's self-designation as a theist, upon his insistence that a scientist can be a theist and need not be a positivist, and upon his statements of what a theist believes.

The first of these statements is part of an effort to show that Comtean positivism is self-contradictory:

> And, then, not being particularly philosophic in temperament, they [Anglo-Saxon disciples of Comte] seek to reconcile themselves to this sceptical state by persuading themselves that theism could offer no rational consolation to its believers, even [if] it could be rationally accepted. Herein they show the secret influence upon them of the capital principle of theism that whatever is is best. (MS 970)

So a Peircean theist, in one respect at least, closely resembles an Hegelian or an Emersonian optimist. Theists are people who hold a certain theoretical view of the world, who are convinced "that they are immortal beings under the government of a loving God" (MS 970)—a somewhat more traditional expression. Because the world is governed by a loving God, whatever is is best. This view, like that William James would later express in *The Will to Believe* (1897), is justified not merely because it is pleasant to hold, but because of the unhappy consequences for one who holds the opposite belief.

After Peirce drew out these implications—life for the pessimist becomes a "weary and purposeless journey"—he provided a more extended definition of theism:

> The capital principle of this is, that nature is absolutely conformed to an end; or in other words, that there is reason in the nature of things. Now from what has been said before it follows that so far as we attain true culture so far will the sum of all our impulses come to the love of the reason as it necessarily is, and therefore so far as we are as we ought to be so are we perfectly gratified by what according to the nature of things, takes place; which is another way of saying that whatever is, is best.... That happens which so far as our own nature is developed, so far as we truly know our own mind, is what delights us most. (MS 970)

We notice first that theism implies a teleological view of nature and of our own lives: recognition of development leads to theism, and life is purposeful. Peirce knew his Hume, so this is not a design argument, but rather a statement of the hypothesis which gives perspective to the theist's view of the world. This hypothesis may also be put: "There is reason in the nature of things." This position, basic to his late "theism," Peirce never abandoned. His cosmological speculation can be read as an attempt to find out how this "reason in the nature of things" works. Already here we see in Peirce a conception of reason both broader and deeper than that of formal logic, or than that of Kant. Peirce continued:

> I know very well that a great many theists are nearer pessimists than optimists but they are unsound and inconsistent. To say, however, that whatever is is best is not to deny the existence of evil, but only to maintain that, if any event is bad in one way it more than counter-balances by being good in another and higher way. (MS 970)

Peirce had not yet adopted Henry James, Sr,'s *Substance and Shadow* (1863) theodicy, in which God creates evil so that there will be something else to love (CP 6.287). This idealistic account would not be difficult to reconcile with the Jamesian approach, if evil were conceived as that element or aspect of reality which consists in its being other than God. It would also be consistent with a Plotinian-Emersonian view of reality as emanating from and returning into the One, a view which Peirce's later writings occasionally suggest (CP 5.119; 1.362).

Peirce then outlined the theory-practice relation with regard to belief in God:

If therefore I am asked as a theist what I have to reply to the arguments of the positivists against religion, I reply in the first place, that positivism is only a particular species of metaphysics open to all the uncertainty of metaphysics and its conclusions are for that reason of not enough weight to disturb any practical belief. We awake to reflection and find ourselves theists. Now those beliefs which come before reflection are generally true, and the reason is that the causes which produce fallacies depend for their operation upon a conscious process of reasoning. But apart from the weight of common sense which must be presumed to attach to theism, the fact that it is my belief itself throws the burden of proof upon its opponents. And metaphysical conclusions ought not in the present state of the science to weigh in practical affairs.

But even if I am asked as a metaphysician whether objections of positivism to religion seem to me to be valid, I still answer not in the least . . . [Peirce then went on to criticize the logic of the verification principle.] (MS 970)

This passage is remarkable for its close resemblance to the doctrine of the 1898 Cambridge lectures, in which Peirce held reasoning to be out of place on vitally important topics. Both are carefully nuanced statements. Peirce was not holding a two-truths theory (CP 6.432)—one for science and scientific metaphysics, one for religious belief and practice. He found in metaphysics no objection to the theism in which he found himself when he awoke to reflection. Nor is this a statement of Mansel's agnosticism, but rather a beginning of a process which would culminate in his late view that instinct is involved in all reasoning, and that reason is a kind of highly refined instinct. Given what Peirce considered an appropriate prejudice in favor of common sense beliefs, he found no reason to suspend theistic belief while working on metaphysics.

Another manuscript of this period, the third of the 1866 Lowell Lectures (MS 354), gives an early statement of a characteristically Peircean argument for theism: God is the hypothesis in an abductive argument:

Every argument by which we get to any truth is also of such a kind as this [hypothetical]. The faculty for this sort of reasoning makes up shrewdness, and is the essence of genius. The alliance of man with the divinity is more plainly seen here than anywhere . . . he observes the finite and he seems to know the possible infinite.

How is it possible that this should be; how can we comprehend such a proceeding? We call such inference, resting upon observation; but when we have drawn seven balls from this bag, we have not observed a single one of the remainder which we infer are all red. So astounding does such a faculty seem; that some logicians have said—it is inspiration and nothing less. . . . For my part, I could not imagine a more sublime manifestation of the Deity than that which thus appears in the nature of inference itself. Nor can I conceive of a function so appropriate to Infinite Power as that of regulating not the universe merely but the very consistencies upon which the possibility of a universe depends. And it seems to me that the power of judging the unseen by this seen . . . affiliates man to the Creator of all things. (MS 354)

The human capacity to frame plausible hypotheses—of evolution, for example—is the best evidence known to Peirce for the reality of a creator. Further, the nature of the creator can be inferred from reflection on the nature of this most amazing of human capacities. If inference is the most "sublime manifestation of the Deity," this strongly Hegelian deity must be something like an immense mind, or like the reasonable, non-arbitrary, character of things which makes such inference possible, or both. Indeed Peirce would often later maintain that regularity, or the law-like character in the universe, is not self-contradictory, but is, above all, that aspect of nature which requires explanation (CP 6.12). He already hints at the continuity between the reasonableness of nature and of the deity.

Still, according to Peirce, "theological logicians" tend to accept this argument but reverse it by holding that "induction rests upon the goodness of God" (MS 354), that is, they think the truth of an inductive inference is guaranteed by God's goodness. These theologians forget that "if the logic rests on theology, theology cannot in its turn rest upon logic. One or the other must be known otherwise than on the testimony of the other." (MS 354) Peirce, willing to use logic as evidence for theism, clearly held inductive logic to be in need of support independent of theology.

He did not, in this lecture, specify what this independent principle might be, and unfortunately some later lectures in the series are missing from the manuscripts. He later developed a theory that induction was self-corrective, and rested its truth upon his theory of reality as that view upon which scientific opinion would converge in the infinite long run if investigation were prolonged. Meanwhile, Peirce thought that those who make logic rest upon theology are logically improvident because they "deprive themselves of the advantage of using Induction and Scientific reasoning generally, as an evidence of the goodness of God." (MS 354)

In the last of the Lowell Lectures on the logic of science for 1866 (CP 7.579-595; MS 359), we find two passages which show the influence of his developing semiotic upon his conception of God. The first finds the sign Jove too vague a symbol even to find a witness or interpretant; the second sees God as the most meaningful of all signs. Peirce had been comparing a man to a word, for example, *six*, and holding them to have the same kind of immortality. He continued:

> This immortality is one which depends on the man's being a true symbol. If instead of *six*, we had written *Jove,* we should have had a symbol which has but a contingent existence; it has no everlasting witness in the nature of things and will pass away or remain only in men's memories without exciting any response in their hearts. It is, indeed, true so far as it means a *supreme being;* its generic soul is true and eternal, but its specific and individual soul is but a shadow. (CP 7.594)

Jove is so vague and general a concept as to be nearly empty. No true symbol, Jove has only contingent historical existence. The true universal—man, six, or the supreme being—finds its interpretant in the specific, the individual, and the concrete. It is not, however, the personal deity whom Peirce relegated to the realm of shadow. This unpublished sequel to CP 7.594 shows the difference:

> There is another important corollary which may be drawn from the law of symbols. As each thing has its symbol, so everything has its symbol. I do not mean the empty conception of *being* the interpretant of absolutely undetermined feeling whose comprehension is *naught;* nor the blind conception of *substance* the interpretant of absolutely undetermined attention. But that symbol whose information is all-embracing; which signifies every fact about everything, not contingently but necessarily. As every soul of man is relative philosophy so this symbol is the absolute unattainable philosophy. This is the Creator of the World since all is necessarily conformed thereto. A personal being for the same reason that all symbols are personal but also further the wellspring of all personality since only by virtue of this Law does the unity of consistency become part of the finite symbol. This infinite Symbol being necessary denotes not the contingent facts of the universe but the absolute law in all its detail and unity to which the universe is subjected, but this law is essentially identical with the Symbol since it is like every fact, the symbol itself. The interpretant of the symbol like every interpretant is also essentially identical with the symbol; and finally the ground of the symbolization or the comprehension of the symbol since it completely determines the symbol in all respects is also essentially identical with it. Here, therefore, we have divine trinity of the object, interpretant, and ground. Each fully constitutes the symbol, and yet all are essential to it. Nor are they the same thing under different points of view but three things which attain identity when the symbol attains infinite information. In many respects this trinity agrees with the Christian trinity; indeed I am not aware that there are any points of disagreement. The interpretant is evidently the Divine Logos or word; and if our former guess that reference to an interpretant is Paternity [CP 7.590] be right, this would

also be the *Son of God*. The ground being that, partaking of which is requisite to any communication with the Symbol, corresponds in its function to the Holy Spirit. I will not, however, carry this speculation any further, as it may be offensive to the prejudices of some who are present. I will only say that, if any one wishes to use this as an argument for the Holy Trinity he must remember that the system of logic must first be accepted upon which it rests. This may conflict with something else he desires to find true. (MS 359)

This passage deserves a careful separate treatment as a starting point for systematic theology or for philosophy of religion, but at this point I will only sketch out the relation of this manuscript to Peirce's emerging conception of God. First of all, God is the symbol of the all, of everything. Peirce had begun this lecture by defining philosophy as the attempt "to form a general informed conception of the All." (CP 7.579) Not the crude pantheism which sees God as the sum of all the sticks and stones, Peirce's logic is a sophisticated inquiry into the sense of experience as a whole. Like Hegel, Peirce recommended "adopting our logic as our metaphysics." (CP 7.680)

Secondly, this symbol of everything is not the empty "Jove" of the earlier passage (CP 7.594), the empty conception whose comprehension is naught, whose character has no practical consequences, but rather is a symbol rich for interpretation. It "signifies every fact about everything" and signifies necessarily. "This is the Creator of the World since all is necessarily conformed thereto." The signifying of this infinite symbol of the All is thus identified with God's creative activity.

Just as a symbol is personal, and every person is a symbol, so is God personal. In fact, God is the infinite source of all personality, of all the finite symbols. God is subject to the ordinary conditions of being a sign, and like every sign, transcends those object-signs. On the other hand, the symbol is fully comprehended in its object, the All, "every fact about everything."

Still, Peirce found a close analogy to traditional Trinitarian doctrines in his conception of God as symbol. Both include in their being the functions of object, interpretant, and ground. Each aspect is fully constitutive of the divine symbol, and all are essential to it. On the face of it, this seems as abstract and empty a conception of God as Jove. Still, in view of his developing propensity to attribute concrete reality to symbols and general ideas—a realism he would proclaim more and more clearly in the coming years—it seems more plausible to take this passage as an indication that Peirce considered God to be at least as real as any other symbol, and surely as real as any other person. Personhood increasingly emerged as an important aspect of Peirce's conception of God. For the moment, he regarded personhood as consisting in the general character of an immortal symbol.

Peirce concluded by reminding us that a theology presupposes a logic, and is no stronger than that logic. Not that logic provides evidence for theology, but theology needs logic, logic adopted as a metaphysics, in order to interpret religious experience.

Peirce went on to provide one of the most interesting and detailed of his many comments on the efficacy of prayer (Cf. MSS 961; 1105; CP 1.660).

> With reference to this conception of the deity it may be asked whether such deity would be a God of Prayer. Here it is necessary to make a distinction between what I shall call spiritual and mechanical prayer. I may illustrate this distinction by comparison with the prayer of a child to its earthly father. Suppose a child to get up on its father's knee and ask to be loved. That would be an instinctive motion connected with an emotion and would certainly find a response in the father's breast. Suppose, again, that a child were to come and make a long harangue to its father, requesting that he would not neglect his paternal duties but would exercise a proper superintendence over its discipline and education, would see its masters were proper persons, and in particular were to take it away from a certain school which the father must already know perfectly well to be an unfit place. In an earthly father, this would scarcely meet with a respectful hearing. With reference to a prayer of the first kind, there can be no doubt that it would find its interpretant in the divine symbol, being an emotion full of truth. An answer it would also receive through the proper chain of material necessary antecedents. On the other hand, the question of the efficacy of the second kind of prayer is altogether a question of fact . . . . (MS 359)

His question here is the conception of God: is this symbol-God a "God of Prayer"? Is it possible for the human personal symbol effectively to contact the divine personal symbol? Peirce opined, as he would again later (CP 6.517; MS 861), that prayer for specifics like rain is inappropriate, even an insult to God comparable to the insult involved in demanding of any loving parent what the child obviously needs. True prayer is putting oneself into an attitude of receptivity, of readiness to be loved and eagerness to learn the truth (MS 434). It is a recognition of one's relation to God (CP 6.516), a dialogic relation, in which either the God-symbol or the human symbol can address the other and can expect to find response.

I conclude that this lecture represented not only an extension of Peirce's early logic to include a semiotic account of personality, but also the early seeds of a highly original philosophical theology. In addition, it shows how closely related Peirce's religious speculations were to the rest of his thought.

Two major outcomes of this early period will appear in the first years of the next period: the "New List of Categories" in 1867, and the *Journal of Speculative Philosophy* articles of 1868, in which Peirce developed and defended his theory that all cognition is inference. I suspect that the tortuous struggle with the place of God in the theory of categories, and with the question of God as an object of faith or of knowledge, may have provided one stimulus to the development of these important papers. Peirce's simplification of Kant's system of categories involved also the elimination of unknowable things-in-themselves, and made the deity knowable. The theory that cognition is inference may have resulted at least partially from his refusal of the faith-reason dichotomy. Whether Peirce was himself satisfied with his treatment of the function of God in a philosophical system is doubtful, but it does seem to me that his early papers contain a whole series of attempts to develop a theistic philosophy. By the end of this period, he saw the human capacity for inference as evidence for a real divinity, and his early semiotic as an argument for the Christian Trinity. Clearly at the end of this period in 1866, Peirce viewed his logic and his philosophical inquiry as enterprises connected to his theism.

Chapter II

THE MIDDLE PERIOD
FROM DESIGN TO DEVELOPMENT

The period 1867-1887 begins with "On a New List of Categories" and the *Journal of Speculative Philosophy* articles of 1868, and ends with the 1887 "Science and Immortality" (CP 6.548-556), published just as the Peirces were moving to Milford, Pennsylvania. During this period Peirce traveled, did a great deal of scientific work, and taught logic at the Johns Hopkins University (1880-1884). His philosophical writings of this period show less direct concern with religious problems than do his earlier and later work, but apart from the *Popular Science Monthly* articles of 1877-1878, evidence of his philosophical work is sparser in this period generally. The two most important pieces for the purposes of this study are "The Order of Nature," the fifth in the 1877-1878 series mentioned above (CP 6.395-427), and an unpublished review of Josiah Royce's *The Religious Aspect of Philosophy,* one draft of which was later published in the *Collected Papers* as CP 8.39-54 (Cf. MS 1369s). Also worth a brief look are a few pre-1878 writings, Peirce's review of F. E. Abbot's *Scientific Theism* (N 1: 71-74), several of the *Century Dictionary* definitions largely written during 1884 and 1885, and "Science and Immortality."

1867 - 1878

As Peirce emerged into what he himself considered his philosophical maturity, he concluded the third of his 1868 articles in the *Journal of Speculative Philosophy* (CP 5.318-357) by linking logic to a social interest (CP 5.354; cf. 2.654), "a transcendent and supreme interest" (CP 5.357) in the "ideal perfection of knowledge by which we have seen that reality is constituted" (CP 5.356), the reality to be discovered in unlimited communal inquiry. He made no direct theistic claims here, but used much religious language to discuss the scientist's unselfish commitment to truth. "But just the *revelation* of the possibility of this complete *self-sacrifice* in man, and the belief in its *saving power,* will serve to *redeem* the logicality of all men." (CP 5.356; emphasis mine) And "he who would not sacrifice his own soul to save the whole world, is illogical in all his inferences, collectively." (CP 5.354) Peirce later identified God, at least partially, with the reasonableness being brought about by the community of inquirers, as well as with the loving and creative relationships in the community which would help this reasonableness to evolve; it seems plausible to see these doctrines in embryo here.

In 1870, Peirce reviewed *The Secret of Swedenborg* by Henry James, Sr. (*North American Review* 110, April 1870, 463-68). He reported, without approval or censure, that James believed God to be necessarily creative, and to be by nature perfect love. God has made creatures for their own sakes, and has given them the illusion of independence. None of this, Peirce noted, had been scientifically established, and indeed, James did not believe his views could be established by reasoning, but rather only by the "sanction of the heart." This view, according to Peirce, deprived James of the right to call his work philosophy. "Religion may be made to rest on religious faith, and a philosophical justification may be given of such a procedure; but it fails to be philosophy while it appeals not to the head, but only to the heart." (p. 465) Peirce may have agreed with the views of James: the book afforded him, he noted, "much spiritual nutriment." (p. 468) Still, he realized, even at this stage, that if he wanted to claim any philosophical status for his own "theism," it would have to stand open to scientific inquiry and philosophical criticism.

Near this same time, an undated manuscript (MS 696) entitled "Practical Maxims of Logic," possibly intended for a series of lectures at Harvard in 1870, contains his longest discussion of the ontological argument. The context is a question about the extent to which all deductive arguments are question-begging. In fact, "if a syllogism which seems to advance our knowledge does not beg the question, it's usually because it has four terms." As an example he cited Anselm's proof for the existence of God. He first presented Anselm's own formulation, then the objection Anselm attributed to Gaunilo, "in favor of the fool," together with Anselm's own response to Gaunilo. Peirce then proceeded to give his own view of the strongest attack and defense of the argument.

Against Anselm's argument, Peirce suggested that it presumes that existence is an essential property, not an accident, of deity, and thus falls into the fallacy of four terms. What Peirce apparently meant is that "that than which nothing greater can be thought" is equivocal: hypothetical in the first premise, and including necessary existence in the second. A parallel case would be the definition of the word *Buz* as a "flaming dragon which has the singular property of appearing to the sight as soon as it is written down." The problem is that when *B-u-z* is written down, no dragon appears. In other words, the argument turns on a misunderstanding of the essentially hypothetical character of all definitions:

> Anything would exist if it did exist. And what a thing would be if it did exist is all that a definition can assert. The argument, therefore, rests upon a confusion between *would be* and *is*, between *being thought* and *being*. (MS 696)

The only defense of the argument must deny that being-thought and really-being can be distinguished in God's case. Peirce opined that support for this claim must rest on a theory of truth. If I say that it is true that there is a statue of Daniel Webster in front of the State House, I mean that *if* I were to go there, I would find an overwhelming amount of evidence in favor of the theory of such a statue's existence, but not some kind of absolute certitude.

> If therefore, a hypothesis is required, an indefinitely large number of facts or as many as you please being taken into account, that constitutes the truth of the hypothesis.
>   Now if we take up that sophism about a flaming dragon we see at once that the *name* Buz was required only in an ideal state of things and therefore has no actual validity. In the theological argument, it is quite different. That an ideal of God is required to bring our general conceptions to unity is admitted on all hands. And that ideal God would not be such unless it were regarded as having existence and therefore it constitutes an hypothesis and as this hypothesis is required in every state of cognition, its truth is constituted theory. (MS 696)

In other words, Anselm's mistake lay in not recognizing the hypothetical character of his ideal God, in not seeing his definition as a mere definition. God is the conclusion of a transcendental argument from the need of all cognitional states, and from the need for unity of thought, and thus must be regarded as the most basic of all hypotheses. But unlike the certain conclusions of syllogistic arguments which can provide no new knowledge, this conclusion, like that of any argument which purports to yield new knowledge, must be held as fallible, as hypothetical. "Its truth is constituted theory"—not fact.

Lest Peirce's account of the argument be construed as merely sceptical, however, it should be noted that the final paragraph quoted above purports to answer the "sophism" of the flaming dragon, and that its general tone rather strongly favors the hypothesis of God's reality. To say that a statement is hypothetical is not to say that it false, or even probably false.

Peirce's 1871 review of Fraser's *The Works of Berkeley* contains nothing directly pertinent to the growth of Peirce's conception of God, but it does include the first full-blown version of Peircean realism (Fisch, 1967). Since reality, as distinguished from mere fiction, later became one of his main affirmations about the deity, I will note a few characteristics of Peirce's view of reality. Reality is mainly to be distinguished from fiction (CP 8.12), and is the opinion which will ultimately be recognized as true in the long run. In addition a reality is the "immediate object of thought in a true judgment" (CP 8.16); it is the truth there to be "found out," the object of scientific inquiry and discovery. Reality is thus not restricted to the being of particulars. Above all, reality has a social character: what is true will be found out and assented to in and by the *community* of inquirers, and is independent of the thoughts of individuals (CP 8.12-13). All these properties of the real bear on Peirce's later claim to believe in the reality of God. In fact, he said in 1893, "I do not believe that anything (unless it be God) quite fulfills the idea of the real." (CP 2.532) This statement, of course, depends on a conception of grades of reality, which is more characteristic of Peirce's later writings, but which is already implicit in a view of reality as something being discovered. It may point toward a conception of God as an ideal perfection of knowledge, an idea he hinted at in the treatment of Anselm's argument, and one which appears clearly as early as 1878.

The Order of Nature

In 1878, Peirce published "The Order of Nature" as the fifth of his six "Illustrations of the Logic of Science" for the *Popular Science Monthly* (CP 6.395-427). This same series began with his "The Fixation of Belief" and "How to Make Our Ideas Clear," in which he outlined and illustrated the distinctive character of scientific thought and introduced the pragmatic maxim. "The Order of Nature" asks whether nature does indeed exhibit order, and what a positive or negative answer to this question might mean for religious belief and practice. This is Peirce's most extended consideration of the design argument as a "fundamental problem in the theory of reasoning": "how we are to think of the ensemble of things." (CP 6.397)

Peirce began by laying down the challenge. If nature is found to be remarkably ordered, science will have to admit consideration of such hypotheses as might explain the universal presence of such order, hypotheses such as "the existence of a governor of the universe" (CP 6.395). Without positive evidence for such an hypothesis, for the necessity of a world-orderer to account for the laws of nature, nothing in favor of the religious hypothesis will "weigh very much with minds emancipated from the tyranny of tradition."

But Peirce distinguished. Some of the world's religions, he noted, are not theistic, or do not postulate an actually existing Deity. In addition, the European thinker Etienne Vacherot finds it reasonable to worship the non-existent "Perfect, the Supreme Ideal," and in fact finds ideality and "real existence" incompatible:

> In fact, M. Vacherot finds it agreeable to his reason to assert that non-existence is an essential character of the perfect, just as St. Anselm and Descartes found it agreeable to theirs to assert the opposite. I con-

fess that there is one respect in which either of these positions seems to me more congruous with the religious attitude than that of a theology which stands upon evidences; for as soon as the Deity presents himself to either Anselm or Vacherot, and manifests his glorious attributes, whether it be in a vision of the night or day, either of them recognizes his adorable God, and sinks upon his knees at once; whereas the theologian of evidences will first demand that the divine apparition shall identify himself, and only after having scrutinized his credentials and weighed the probabilities of his being found among the totality of existences will he finally render his circumspect homage, thinking that no characters can be adorable but those which belong to a real thing. (CP 6.396; Vacherot, 1869)

The first thing to be noticed about this ironic passage, especially in view of the opinion Peirce expressed later in the same article that "the spirit of science is hostile to any religion except such a one as that of M. Vacherot" (CP 6.426), is that he spoke quite approvingly of Vacherot's position, and was thus not himself hostile to all religion at this period (Mahowald, 1976: 367-77). He found the proponents of the design argument, the theologians of evidences by whom he was taught at Harvard, themselves lacking in the religious attitude. Sceptical of Anselm's argument (MS 1596), he found himself being offered a whole new conception of a Deity, perhaps not open to the same criticisms as those he himself would bring against the classical proofs of a traditionally existent God who orders and governs the universe.

Given Peirce's later insistence on the reality of ideals, we might suppose him beginning already to distinguish between the reality and the existence of God, but since he continued to use "existence" in regard to God even as late as 1892 (CP 6.162), it is highly improbable that he was really using this distinction in 1878. His use here of "real existence" and "real being" support reasonable doubt that this distinction operates here; in fact "reality" seems in the context to mean what he will later call Secondness or existence.

But we have here at least a suggestion of the later rejection of God's existence in favor of God's reality. Peirce rather scornfully accused the theologian of evidences of having reduced God to an item in the universe of existences. The deity of Vacherot, on the contrary, the Perfect, the Supreme Ideal, need not already exist, in fact must not yet exist. It would hardly make sense to fall on one's knees and adore an item in the world.

In Book II, Chapter V of *La Religion,* cited by Peirce as source of the idea "that the very notion of the Ideal is repugnant to its real existence" (CP 6.396), Vacherot argues that philosophy is the mature form of religion without its theologies, dogmas, and cult. Religion, in an individual or in a culture, is a youthful, imagination-dependent state of mind. In adulthood it is replaced by philosophy, which worships the ideal and recognizes that this perfection is the same thing religion seeks imaginatively. Imagination, he thought, should restrict itself to its proper domain in poetry and art.

"L'idéal religieux; c'est le suprême exemplaire de toute perfection. Symboles à part, n'est-ce pas là aussi l'idéal philosophique?" (Vacherot, 1869: 286) Though the religious and philosophical ideas correspond, the religious sentiment recognizes only the realized ideal, while the philosopher can admire the ideal itself. Where Peirce differed from Vacherot was in believing that the practice of religion can make sense without adherence to its dogmas (CP 6.427): Peirce would not reject the celebration of Christmas and Easter as belonging "à l'âge de l'enfance and de la jeunesse." (Vacherot, 1869: 308)

In fact in CP 6.396 Peirce used the presence or absence of a religious attitude to evaluate conceptions of God, and to criticize arguments for the existence of such deities. In pragmatic fashion, conduct—religious or not—was being used to evaluate theory.

Peirce also repeatedly accused theologians of not believing in the efficacy of prayer, since they would not allow it to be tested scientifically. When John Tyndall had proposed that the clergy refrain from praying for rain in certain districts, so that the results of this abstention could be measured, they refused and called his suggestion blasphemous (MS 891). Peirce believed that the efficacy or non-efficacy of praying for specific results was a scientific question, and the clergy's reluctance to see it tested was, for him, pragmatic proof only of their sceptical attitude toward their own religion (Cf. CP 6.515; 1.660).

Finally, the question which puzzled Peirce in 1892 (CP 6.162), and which would receive extended treatment in 1908 (CP 6.452-493), arises in embryo here. In what does religious knowledge consist? Is God the conclusion of some inductive reasoning? Or, as Anselm and Descartes would have it, does a deity follow deductively from an analysis of definitions? Peirce speaks approvingly of those who "recognize" their adorable God. Such talk is quite congruent with the view of the later Peirce who would invite people to muse, to reflect, and thus to experience the beauty of the hypothesis of God's reality. The recognition then may consist in the matching of a hypothetical conception of God with one's own religious experience.

The central sections of "The Order of Nature" consist of detailed arguments for Peirce's conclusion that the world is more ordered than disordered, but not nearly orderly enough to justify the inference of an orderer outside the universe itself. First of all, any randomly selected collection of objects will have some common character (CP 6.402). These commonalities, or uniformities, or regularities may not be interesting to us, and indeed careful attention to these regularities would show us a universe "with such an air of system that there would be nothing to ask" and in which "no action of ours, and no event of Nature would have important consequences." (6.406) A world of chance is "our actual world viewed from the standpoint of an animal at the very vanishing point of intelligence." Peirce concluded that "thus, nothing can be made out from the orderliness of nature in regard to the existence of a God, unless it be maintained that the existence of a finite mind proves the existence of an infinite one." (CP 6.407)

In the section entitled "Induction," he countered Mill's view that the validity of induction depends on the uniformity of Nature by an appeal to the observation already noted that common characters can always be found in randomly selected groups, and that most of these uniformities are highly uninteresting. Induction, however, requires that the character to be noted be designated in advance of research, and to ignore this condition is to deprive the "uniformity of Nature" hypothesis of any interest, since it could not be disconfirmed (CP 6.413). As a result, the order of Nature does not explain the success of induction or anything else.

Peirce was, however, interested in accounting for the tendency of human minds to make correct inferences. After a brief bow to fallibilism—"that we ever do discover the precise causes of things, that any induction is absolutely without exception, is what we have no right to assume" (CP 6.416), he noted that certain inductions, such as the conceptions of space and time, approach such an extraordinary universality that "we cannot possibly think that they have been reached merely by accident." (CP 6.416) It seemed to him then that the whole development of mind must have depended on the strong adaptation of the human mind to the comprehension of the world (CP 6.417). This adaptation, the result of natural selection, is the answer to Kant's question about how science is possible. Science is possible because it is needed for preservation of the species. The accuracy with which the conception of space, time and mass describe the world made Peirce suspect "some secret here which remains to be discovered." (CP 6.418)

Finally Peirce took up the design question directly. If the universe is infinite, to claim that some design beyond the knowing power of all intellects exists is to assert "an absolutely incognizable existence"—a nonsensical phrase (CP 6.419). The conception of God Peirce rejected here was a conflation of the Kantian noumenal God with the God whose existence he took to be the conclusion of the design argument. Now reasons can be found for viewing the universe as finite and susceptible of a single explanation, or as infinite (CP 6.420-421), but such reasons he found inconclusive. Peirce settled at this time for viewing the universe as "too vast to have any character" (CP 6.422), and as a result, too vast to justify any inference to a plan or design. Thus, "it would be extravagant to say that science can at present disprove religion, but it does seem to me that the spirit of science is hostile to any religion except such a one as that of M. Vacherot." (CP 6.426) This is, however, a very important "except"; Peirce's critique was of empiricist approaches to theological questions. His pragmatism and his idealism left him other options.

The concluding paragraphs of "The Order of Nature" focus on the practical effects of the criticism of the design argument. The clergy condemn Buddhism, which, like Vacherot's doctrine, does not assert the real existence of a deity, for its presumed adverse effects on morality and on the belief in the efficacy of prayer. In the face of such objections, Peirce appealed to the fundamental obligation to seek truth:

> Let the consequences of such a belief be as dire as they may, one thing is certain: that the state of the facts, whatever it may be, will surely get found out, and no human prudence can long arrest the triumphal car of truth, no, not if the discovery were such as to drive every individual of our race to suicide! (CP 6.426)

Still, since religion does not depend on acceptance of the conclusion of the design argument, these dire consequences are unlikely to ensue.

> It would be folly to suppose that any metaphysical theory in regard to *the mode of being of the perfect* is to destroy that *aspiration toward the perfect* which constitutes the essence of religion. (CP 6.427, emphasis mine)

Indeed, people with various philosophical views generally believe the really fundamental principles of Christianity, Peirce thought, and ought not to be excluded from worship. Religion itself is "aspiration toward the perfect." In other words, Peirce in 1878 accepted Vacherot's conception of God as the perfect, or as the supreme ideal, together with Vacherot's conviction that such a deity may be an object of worship.

ROYCE's *Religious Aspect of Philosophy* (1885)

In 1885 Josiah Royce published *The Religious Aspect of Philosophy,* and Peirce wrote a long review intended for, but not accepted by, *Popular Science Monthly*. Three versions of this review survive. The longest has been published as CP 8.39-54; two others, from both of which pages seem to be missing, and one of which is very short, are catalogued by Robin as MS 1369s. Both the longer drafts contain material which sheds light on the development of Peircean theism. Both compare Peirce's and Royce's conceptions of idealism, the real, and God.

The review published in the *Collected Papers* begins by considering Royce's claim that the reality of error, together with the inability of one who is in error simultaneously to recognize the mistake and to hold it, implies the existence of a God whose thought is what we mean by the truth. In other words, "the reality of whatever really exists consists in the real thing being thought by God." (CP 8.40) Against this view Royce had cited the position of a certain Thrasymachus—Peirce took this as an insulting reference to his own views—who had suggested that "reality, the fact that there is such a thing as a true answer to a question" (CP 8.41), is the ultimate outcome of inquiry, what anyone would believe in the long run. The variant reads:

Dr. Royce's particular variety of idealism is that the real is what God has in his consciousness. Here is a logical and a theological proposition in one. Confining our attention first to the logical doctrine; it is that truth consists in the agreement of our judgments with an absolute thought. Dr. Royce strongly insists that this thought must be that of an actual, living, conscious, being. A certain writer has suggested that whether there be a living being whose thought coincides with this absolute thought or not, the latter only becomes the standard toward which human science, with its methods of experiment and reasoning, is ultimately tending, so that it is the goal which sufficient investigation would reach. . . . (MS 1369s)

Peirce did not deny the accuracy of Royce's Hegelian conception of God; he simply spelled out its pragmatic meaning. Perhaps too Peirce, for whom the ideal and the real will ultimately coincide, was even more an idealist than Royce. Royce apparently took Peirce's "would believe" in a very weak sense. "No barely possible judge," Peirce accurately quoted him as saying, "who *would* see the error, *if* he were there, will do for us." (CP 8.41; Royce, 1885: 427; emphasis Royce's)

Peirce's first response, and for the present inquiry his most interesting one, is as follows:

Yet if I were to present Dr. Royce as preferring to believe for a little while that which a certain Being—no matter who—imagines, rather than to come at once to the belief to which investigation is destined to carry him, I should probably be doing him injustice; because I suppose he would say that the thing which God imagines, and the opinion to which investigation would ultimately lead him, in point of fact, coincide. If, however, these two things coincide, I fail to understand why he should be so cruel to the childish Thrasymachus; since after all, there is no real difference between them, but only a formal one,—each maintaining as a theorem that which the other adopts as a definition. (CP 8.41)

Although Peirce added some remarks about the Hegelians' neglect of Secondness, or the role of the will in cognition, the point to be noted is Peirce's basic agreement with Royce. He could not understand why Royce did not see that they were in the same camp, unless the problem was Royce's weak concept of possibility. Peirce's final upshot of investigation is no more a "*barely* possible judge" (CP 8.43) than Royce's God was. Granted that Peirce's judge lacks infallible certainty, since "the final opinion which would be sure to result from sufficient investigation may possibly, in reference to a given question, never be actually attained, owing to a final extinction of intellectual life or for some other reason." (CP 8.43) Still this ideal final opinion is real. In fact many beliefs have already been settled, and "our experience in this direction warrants us in saying with the highest degree of empirical confidence that questions that are either practical or could conceivably become so are susceptible of receiving final solutions provided the existence of the human race be indefinitely prolonged and the particular question excite sufficient interest." (CP 8.43) For Peirce, this was the pragmatic meaning of God's omniscience; whether God or human investigators ever find answers to questions without conceivable practical bearings he did not care, since such questions mean nothing.

He admitted, for the sake of argument, that some meaningful questions may forever escape being actually answered. But that there are questions which in principle can never be answered is an opinion which depends on a faulty conception of reality; "an unknowable reality is nonsense." (CP 8.43) We thus proceed as if all our questions will eventually have answers.

Peirce did go on to formulate Royce's theory of God's omniscience in these terms: "the real existence of God would consist in his imagination or positing Himself; it would thus be according to him, of the same nature as the reality of anything else." (CP 8.44) Peirce refrained from commenting on this view except to note that his own was different:

> I think that the existence of God, as well as we can conceive of it consists in this, that a tendency toward ends is so necessary a constituent of the universe that the mere action of chance upon innumerable atoms has an inevitable teleological result. One of the ends so brought about is the development of intelligence and of knowledge; and therefore I should say that God's omniscience, humanly conceived, consists in the fact that knowledge in its development leaves no question unanswered. The scepticism just spoken of about the actual answer to every question would admit this omniscience as a regulative but not a speculative conception. I believe that even that view is more religiously fruitful than the opinion of Dr. Royce. (CP 8.44)

This statement of "another theory" is the first of many the later Peirce made using teleological conceptions of God, evolution, and creation. God is the "somewhere" that the universe is going. It may be asked, of course, did he not then sneak the design argument back into his thought? Perhaps, but with a new twist. Instead of inferring a designer from an apparent design, Peirce simply here identified God with the "tendency towards ends"—one of his strongest immanence-statements. This immanence, however, consists in creative involvement in the evolution of intelligence and knowledge, not in simply being identified with the product-universe.

In addition, Peirce again evaluated—as he had in 1878—a conception and an attribute of the deity by using the pragmatic test of influence upon religious conduct.

In the second section of the review, in the course of criticizing the early Royce's Hegelian methodology as applied to moral distinctions, Peirce provided another undeveloped and elusive clue to his 1885 idea of God. An ordinary clear-headed person will say:

> ... right and wrong are nothing to me except so far as they are connected with certain rules of living by which I am enabled to satisfy a real impulse which works in my heart; and this impulse is the love of my neighbor elevated into a love of an ideal and divine humanity which I identify with the providence which governs the world. (CP 8.47)

Taking this statement together with that quoted above from 8.44, it is not too difficult to hear the accents of the Peirce who, seven years later, would expound upon God as evolutionary love. The reality which comes eventually to be known is the ideal loved and identified with Providence. The ends and ideas were perhaps still, in 1885, contained within the world-process, along with the "existence of God" and the "providence which governs the world." Not until the turn of the century would Peirce clearly suggest that ideals themselves partially transcend the processes for which they are ends or purposes.

In summary, Peirce's comments on Royce's book show that he had done some thinking on religious questions since 1878, and especially that consideration of theories of evolution had influenced his thinking. Evolution led Peirce, not to the rejection of religion, nor to attempts to reconcile religion and science, but rather to reinterpretations of common views of God and of creation.

OTHER PRE-MILFORD WRITINGS

A few other writings of this period provide clues to the character of Peirce's view of God in the 1880s. In a manuscript entitled "One, Two, Three" (MS 901s, c. 1885), in the context of a discussion of mathematical conceptions of an absolute, he suggested that there are three possible ways to conceive of the possibility of a metaphysical absolute:

> If the universe never advances or develops at all, or if there is merely an alternate flow and ebb of progress then there is no absolute in creation. If, as the pessimists maintain, the character of its growth is such that it tends in the infinite future to come out at the same non-entity from which it has [been?] proceeding since an infinite past, that infinitely distant state of Nirvana is the single Absolute. But if as evolutionists believe, it has been since infinity leaving a state of absolute homogeneity and is tending forever toward another different state of absolute organized heterogeneity, there is a double absolute. (MS 901s; cf. MS 904)

It is this "Absolute organized heterogeneity" that Peirce in the 1890s would identify with "concrete reasonableness," and at times, with God. Perhaps the evolutionary process itself became for Peirce a kind of argument for the reality of God.

In 1886, Peirce reviewed *Scientific Theism,* by his friend Francis Ellingwood Abbot. Abbot had reasoned from actual knowledge of the universe to its infinite intelligibility, and from there, by nine steps, to a conception of the universe as "Infinite Person, Absolute Spirit, Creative Source and Eternal Home of the derivative finite personalities which depend upon it, but are no less real than itself." (N 1: 71) Peirce opined that if the conclusion really followed from the premises, there ought to be a shorter proof. In ten steps, he thought, reason was likely to have stumbled, as it did immediately in inferring infinite knowability from actual knowledge. In addition Peirce criticized Abbot's book for its "energetic dualism." "Everything like uniting the members of his main distinction by insensible gradations, by a deeper underlying unity, or by any mediating cause, except the Divine mind which creates the relations but not the related things, is foreign to his idea." (N 1: 72) Peirce's complaint, a critique by a first-rate scientist and mathematician, has undertones of an early "synechism" (continuity-philosophy): he finds Abbot "remarkably loathe to admit mediation . . . ." There are also echoes of the realism of the Royce review:

> . . . although science must hold the facts it discovers to be independent of the opinion of any person or persons, it by no means follows that it need insist on their being independent of the final upshot of sufficient investigation, nor that it need hold them to be independent of the creative thought of the Deity. (N 1: 74)

Reflection on Royce had taught Peirce that his "final upshot" and the "creative thought of the Deity" were nearly, if not completely, equivalent. Reflection on evolutionary theories had taught him that God's creative action must be both teleological and immanent in evolutionary processes themselves.

Last in order of publication (1889-1891), but earlier in order of study and writing (mostly 1884-1886), were Peirce's many definitions for the *Century Dictionary*. This task forced Peirce into a great deal of reading and rereading in the history of philosophy, and also into the clarification of many of his ideas. Many of the philosophical definitions relate in one way or another to Peirce's religious views. I will quote and comment on a few definitions of particular interest for my search for his conception of God, bearing in mind that his task was to report usage, not to create it.

The Absolute, in metaphysics, is "(a) that which is free from any restriction, or is unconditioned; hence, the ultimate ground of all things; God: as, it is absurd to place a limit to the power of the Absolute. (b) that which is perfect or complete: as, its beauty approaches the absolute. (c) That which is independent of some or all relations; the non-relative." The first two definitions, taken together, suggest that Peirce may have closely connected the idea of the "perfect" or "perfection" with that of the Absolute, and that his later affirmations of belief in the Absolute may carry more or less the same meaning as his earlier talk of religion as "aspiration toward the perfect." (CP 6.427)

Philosophies of the absolute are "certain systems of metaphysics founded on Kant's *Critique of Reason*—most prominently those of Fichte, Schelling, and Hegel—which departing from the principles of Kant, maintain that the absolute is cognizable," that is, does not belong to a noumenal realm. A few years later Peirce called himself a modified Schellingian (MS 958), and he had long insisted that no reality is incognizable.

Other interesting definitions are of creation and of creationism:

Creation: The act of creating or causing to exist; especially the act of producing both the material and the form of that which is made; production from nothing; specifically the original formation of the universe by the Deity.

Creationism: The doctrine that matter and all things were created, substantially as they now exist, by the fiat of an omnipotent Creator, and not gradually evolved or developed: opposed to evolutionism.

Peirce was by this time clearly opposed to creationism as he here defined it. In his 1884 address on "Design and Chance," he had characterized Epicurus as holding that

... divineness comes from a special cause and does not originate by chance from elements not containing it. Darwin's view is nearer to mine. Indeed my opinion is only Darwinism analyzed, generalized, and brought into the realm of Ontology. (MS 875)

In fact this definition of creation seems a good example of his reporting usage as opposed to legislating it. For his own philosophical vocabulary, he was just in the process of developing new meanings for the word creation (CP 6.302; MS 958)

A definition which provides links with both Peirce's earlier and his later work is that of *infinite*. Its first and mathematical definition is: "immeasurable or innumerably great; so great as to be absolutely incapable of being measured or counted." Second, the infinite is the "all-embracing; lacking nothing; the greatest possible; perfect; absolute; applied only to Divinity." Peirce had attributed this conception of the deity to Anselm and to Vacherot in 1878. Whether he was now ready to commit himself on the issue of "real existence" is unclear. All definitions, he claimed, are hypothetical.

What is clear is that the infinite is the inclusive. If there is an infinite being, that being includes everything in the universe. Just after the definition cited above, he quoted the following from Mansel's *Limits of Religious Thought:*

> That which is conceived as absolute and *infinite* must be conceived as containing within itself the sum not only of all actual, but of all possible modes of being.

Must an inclusive deity be pantheistic then? Not for Peirce. To say that a being, even a hypothetical one, includes the sum of other things is not to say that that being is *nothing but* the sum of those other beings. Rather it is to hold that a being must be *at least* such a container. Peirce defined "immanence" (below) very carefully.

The definitions of *pantheism, pantheist, cosmotheism,* and *immanence* show how sensitive Peirce was to the issues involved.

> *Pantheism:* 1. The worship of all the gods. 2. The metaphysical doctrine that God is the only substance, of which the material universe and man are only manifestations. It is accompanied with a denial of God's personality. Pantheism is essentially unchristian; and the word implies rather the reprobation of the speaker than any very definite opinion [Cf. N 1: 164].
>
> *Pantheist:* One who holds the doctrine of pantheism; one who believes that God and the universe are identical.
>
> *Cosmotheism:* Deification of the cosmos; the system which identifies God with the cosmos; pantheism.
>
> *Immanent:* . . . In modern philosophy the word is applied to the operations of a creator conceived as in organic connection with the creation, and to such a creator himself, as opposed to a *transient or transcendent* creating and creator from whom the creation is conceived as separated. The doctrine of an immanent deity does not necessarily imply that the world, or the soul of the world, is God, but only that it either is or is in God.

The most interesting aspect of this set of definitions is the way they differentiate between pantheism and immanentism. Pantheism simply identifies the world and God, is unchristian, and is an insult to an opponent, a "dirty word" (Lauer, 1979). The definition of immanence, on the contrary, a very carefully nuanced description of one way of conceiving the God-world relationship, has a tone of respectability. Immanentism, unlike pantheism, has its deity involved in an evolutionary process. Remembering Peirce's 1884 claim to be generalizing Darwin, and looking forward to his 1892 conception of God as evolutionary love (CP 6.287-317), I suspect that he considered himself an immanentist in the late 1880s, and perhaps throughout the 1890s.

In 1887, in a small piece entitled "Science and Immortality," Peirce proclaimed what he called "the breakdown of the mechanical philosophy." Evolutionary studies had made it clear that the world is not governed by blind law, so it seemed to Peirce reasonable to consider more "spiritualistic" views on various matters, such as the possibility of a future life (CP 6.555). Such a doctrine had surely not yet been confirmed by evidence, but there was no reason "why the dwellers on earth should not, in some future day, find out for certain whether there is a future life or not." The scientist does not antecedently decide such questions, but remains ready to examine all questions. The scientist does not disparage any kind of speculation.

At the end of Peirce's very early work, he was an avowed theist trying to make philosophical sense of his theism. Between 1867 and 1887, his efforts to work out the "religious difficulties suggested by scientific ideas" (MS 1367) were most often bound up with explanations of his realism. God was the ideal, the perfect, at least minimally transcendent because still up ahead, but especially the immanent and the all-inclusive. In conceiving creation, the emphasis shifted from design to development. In the 1880s, Peirce began to explore the non-deterministic implications of evolutionary theory for a possible theism, and to look for explanations of growth from chaos to cosmos. By the middle 1880s, he had read Cantor and was fascinated by the possible usefulness of conceptions of continuity for an evolutionary cosmology. Above all, evolution suggested to him a teleological view of the world which corresponded to his earlier goal-seeking conception of cognition. He was ready to make a guess at the cosmological riddle.

Chapter III

THE EARLY ARISBE YEARS

In the first thirteen of his years at "Arisbe" in Milford, Pennsylvania (1887-1900), Peirce's conception of God became enriched by two major developments in his philosophy. In the late 1880s and early 1890s, he presented, in the unfinished and unpublished "A Guess at the Riddle" (CP 1.354-416) and in the five *Monist* articles of 1892-1893, the evolutionary cosmology he had been developing since 1884 (Fisch, 1971: 198). The major philosophical outlook which formed this cosmology he called "synechism" or the philosophy of continuity. Near the end of the century, he began to pay attention to what he called the normative sciences, and in the process the earlier "Perfect" and the Ideal of Knowledge became identified with the *summum bonum* of evolving concrete reasonableness.

This period provides a wealth of material for the study of Peirce's developing theism, but much of it is unfinished. In this chapter therefore, instead of considering the papers and manuscripts in a strictly chronological fashion, I will break the period into two sub-periods. Within each shorter period, I will first consider religious themes which seem most continuous and consistent with his earlier work, then examine new elements and emphases.

1890 - 1894

Much of what Peirce said of God in the early 1890s appears as the direct outgrowth of his previous decade's thought on categories, and on the related evolutionary cosmology. In fact, Peirce himself saw it so. In "A Guess at the Riddle" (1889 and 1890), in the course of his experiment at applying his triadic conceptions to various branches of science, he gave an account, frustratingly enigmatic, of his philosophical development in the 1880s. He had worked, he explained, on applying his categories to logic, psychology, physiology, the biology of protoplasm, natural selection, and

Epicurean physics (Fisch, 1971: 190-192), "the exploration of which long prevented my looking further."

> As soon, however, as I was induced to look further, and to examine the application of the three ideas to the deepest problems of the soul, nature and God, I saw at once that they must carry me far into the heart of those primeval mysteries. (CP 1.364)

It was then, work on the categories, together with his discovery of continuity as the "master key" (MS 949) to philosophical problems, which led Peirce back into the classical metaphysical problems which had so fascinated him in his college years. He approached them now with more sophistication, having learned from Vacherot and Royce. And his conception of God as ideal or absolute end of knowledge grew to include the Absolute as end of the evolutionary process. About 1892, however, striking new elements appear right in the middle of the *Monist* series. All at once Peirce began to identify the metaphysical Absolute with the God who is the object of religious experience. The later articles in the series treat the concepts of individual and corporate personality, and speculate on the knowledge of a personal God.

Let us turn first to those elements of the writings of the early 1890s which exhibit most continuity with the writings of the middle period. Peirce continued to imply that, even though the disparate methods of science and theology put them at odds, and must continue to do so until theology gives up its infallibilism, still the truth in which religious people believe and that which scientists seek to discover are not two truths but one. Since, then, there is no nonreligious reality, science is the discovery of God. "Many great scientists go to church, and are there very unlike what they are in their laboratories. At one time they are studying one aspect of truth, at another time another." (N 1: 155) He claimed to be "sure that truth is not split into two warring doctrines." (CP 6.432)

This is consistent with Peirce's insistence in 1885 that his conception of God's omniscience—the ideal perfection of knowledge to be expected as the result of endless inquiry—was not so very different from Royce's view that truth is what God thinks. In the course of his efforts to use the conceptions of continuity and of continuous evolution to overcome philosophical dualisms such as mind/matter, and self/non-self, he re-emphasized this one-truth view by referring repeatedly to the affinity he found between human minds and the mind of God. In distinguishing three forms of agapastic evolution, for example, in "Evolutionary Love," he suggested that an idea

> ... may affect an individual, independently of his human affections, by virtue of an attraction it exercises upon his mind, even before he has comprehended it. This is the phenomenon which has well been called

> the *divination* of genius; for it is due to the continuity between the man's mind and the Most High. (CP 6.307; cf. MS 957)

On the other hand, we are warned to be critical of the specific contents of inspiration:

> The divine mind is inscrutable; the purposes of God cannot be fathomed. How can we tell that he would not choose to inspire a man with a false belief,—especially when we see that he has allowed the most hideous corruptions to taint every church and every religion. (MS 862)

Peirce would more often attribute such corruptions to the failure to recognize the fallibility of those who receive revelation, but here he seems to impute them to the divine mind itself.

Peirce also continued throughout this period to call God the Absolute. God is the Alpha and Omega, the Absolute beginning and the Absolute end of everything: this is the evolutionary view proclaimed in "A Guess at the Riddle":

> The starting point of the universe, God the Creator is the Absolute First; the terminus of the universe, God completely revealed, is the Absolute Second; every state of the universe at a measureable point of time is the third . . . . if your creed is that the whole universe is approaching in the infinitely distant future a state having a general character different from that toward which we look back in the infinitely distant past, you make the absolute to consist in two distinct real points and are an evolutionist. (CP 1.362; cf. 6.27)

God is not merely the mathematical, nor even the metaphysical, absolute here—the infinite which makes sense of the finite. God is the cosmological beginning, the creative spontaneity in the original chaos of feeling, and the ideal outcome of the evolutionary process. Religion then becomes in the individual

> . . . a sort of sentiment, or obsure perception, a deep recognition of a something in the circumambient All, which if he strives to express it, will clothe itself in forms more or less extravagant, more or less accidental, but ever acknowledging the first and last, the A and Ω as well as a relation to that Absolute of the individual's self, as a relative being. But religion cannot reside in its totality in a single individual . . . . (CP 6.429)

In this passage from "The Marriage of Religion and Science" (1893), Peirce identified God not as the "circumambient All" but as the "something" which is first and last in the all. That this "something" develops or evolves is clear (NEM 4: 377). In fact these two passages suggest that the reality of the Absolute, its expression in historical process, and our recognition of this evolving reality, all develop.

Peirce gave many accounts of his evolutionary cosmogony. One from "A Guess at the Riddle" runs as follows:

> Out of the womb of indeterminacy we must say there would have come something, by the principle of Firstness, which we may call a flash. Then by the principle of habit there would have been a second flash ... Then there would have come other successions ever more and more closely connected, the habits and the tendency to take them ever strengthening themselves, until the events would have been bound together into something like a continuous flow. (CP 1.412)

The "womb of indeterminacy," the original chaos of chance—Peirce called his doctrine of real chance "tychism"—or spontaneity or Firstness, will soon be accompanied by Secondness, (dyadicity), which will in turn engender substances and laws of nature.

> Pairs of states will also begin to take habits, and thus each state having different habits with reference to the different other states will give rise to bundles of habits, which will be substances. Some of these states will chance to take habits of persistency, and will get to be less and less liable to disappear.... in fact, habits, for the mode of their formation, necessarily consist in the permanency of some relation, and therefore, on this theory, each law of nature would consist in some permanence, such as the permanence of mass, momentum, and energy .... (CP 1.414-415)

In other words, something like Darwinian natural selection has been extended to the entire universe, and the chaos has engendered the cosmos studied by physicists. This process can be expected to continue toward an ultimate end-state in which the indeterminacy has completely acquired form and order.

God became more and more strongly identified for Peirce with this ideal outcome or end of the evolutionary process. In 1868, and in 1878, God had been the ideal perfection of knowledge. Without denying this, he went on in 1885 and in the 1890s to think of God as the reality, the Absolute Second, toward which evolution must be moving. The continued influence of Absolute chance, breaking up matter hidebound with habit, and introducing mental complexity, is moving the universe toward the Absolute Second, God completely revealed. "I do not believe that anything (unless it be God) quite fulfills the idea of the real" (CP 2.532), said Peirce's *Grand Logic* of 1893. Reality and God share the not-yet character of an ideal end only dimly perceived as the outcome of the evolutionary process. Perhaps Peirce's God is indeed the outcome of a transcendental or "abductive" argument: that which would make sense of evolution and inquiry, the 1908 "strictly hypothetical God" of CP 6.467.

This impression that Peirce's God is an abductive, ideal, beginning-and-end receives support from his 1890 article, "Logic and Spiritualism" (CP 6.557-587), which draws heavily on a mathematical metaphor:

> Philosophy tries to understand. In so doing, it is committed to the assumption that things are intelligible, that the process of nature and the process of reason are one. Its explanation must be derivation. Explanation, derivation, involve suggestion of a starting point—starting-point in its own nature not requiring explanation nor admitting of derivation. Also, there is suggestion of goal or stopping-point, where the process of reason and nature is perfected. A principle of movement must be assumed to be universal. It cannot be supposed that things ever reached the stopping-point, for there movement would stop and the principle of movement would not be universal; and similarly with the starting-point. Starting-point and stopping-point can only be ideal, like the two points where the hyperbola leaves one asymptote and where it joins the other. (CP 6.581)

Peirce thus believed, as early as 1890, that scientific philosophy required an assumption that mind and nature are fundamentally one. Since reason needs at least an ideal cosmological beginning and final outcome, whether or not these ideal points have actual existence, we are entitled to suppose them to have at least the kind of reality that we attribute to mathematical ideal limits. We can then use such ideas to estimate the probable truth of other ideas, such as that of telepathy. Peirce called the Alpha-and-Omega idea, or the idea of the double-absolute, the "hyperbolic philosophy" (CP 6.585), and contrasted it with the elliptic and parabolic philosophies, which correspond to the views which consider the beginning and end of the universe to be non-existent and identical, respectively (MS 928; CP 6.27). But even for the hyperbolic philosophy, these points "can only be ideal." Not until later, when he became convinced of the reality of ideals, would Peirce talk much about the reality of God, but he spoke of God as cosmological beginning and/or outcome, to the end of his life.

But this God remains creator, at least in the special sense Peirce gave to the term "creator." God as cherishing-love explains evolution in the last of the 1892-1893 *Monist* articles. "The movement of love is circular, at one and the same time projecting creations into independency and drawing them into harmony" (CP 6.288). This Plotinian-sounding account of creative love may elucidate Peirce's claims, already quoted, to be a New England Transcendentalist or Schellingian (CP 6.102; cf. Perry, 1935 2: 415-416). Growth, or evolution, according to Peirce, comes only from love

(CP 6.289), and this love is not love for an abstraction, but is directed toward those near and dear to us. That Peirce should have chosen, with John's gospel, to identify God with loving and growth-producing relationships between and among human beings, indicates the depth of his commitment to an immanentist conception of God, and also to an idea of God as evolutionary creator. Peirce even compared God's creative activity to his own:

> Suppose, for example, that I have an idea that interests me. It is my creation. It is my creature; for as shown in last July's *Monist* [6.270], it is a little person. I love it, and I will sink myself in perfecting it. It is not by dealing out cold justice to the circle of my ideas that I can make them grow, but by cherishing and tending them as I would the flowers in my garden. The philosophy we draw from John's gospel is that this is the way mind develops; and as for the cosmos, only so far as it yet is mind, and so has life, is it capable of further evolution. Love, recognizing germs of loveliness in the hateful, gradually warms it into life, and makes it lovely. (CP 6.289)

Just as tending and cherishing are necessary to the life and growth of living things, the universe as a whole grows toward reasonableness by being loved—being projected forth from God and drawn back into harmony, a dialectic of independence and unity. Further, the contrast Peirce drew between the gospel of love and the gospel of greed—political economy's "formula of redemption"—suggests that much of this creative loving is located precisely in human relationships. "The gospel of Christ says that progress comes from every individual merging his individuality in sympathy with his neighbors." (CP 6.294)

Above all, Peirce now saw religious experience as necessary for the recognition of the deity, and identified God as that "something" to which religious experience points. A brief biographical parenthesis may serve to introduce this new emphasis. After the move to Milford in 1887, Peirce used to stay in New York City for varying periods of time in the 1890s. During one of these stays, on 24 April 1892, he wrote the following letter to an unidentified correspondent:

> Dear and Reverend Sir:
> I took the Holy Communion at St. Thomas's this morning,—in fact just now,—under peculiar circumstances, which it seems proper to report.
> For many years I have not taken the Communion and have seldom entered a church, although I have always had a passionate love for the church and a complete faith that the essence of christianity, whatever that might be, was Divine; but still I could not reconcile my notions of common sense and of evidence with the proposition of the creed, and I

found going to church made me sophistical and gave me an impulse to play fast and loose with matter of intellectual integrity. Therefore, I gave it up; though it has been the cause of many a bitter reflection. Many times I have tried to cipher out some justification for my return to the communion of the church; but I could not. Especially, the last two nights I have lain awake thinking of the matter.

This morning after breakfast I felt I must go to church anyway. I wandered about, not knowing where to find a regular episcopal church, in which I was confirmed; but I finally came to St. Thomas. I had several times been in it on week days to look at the chancel. I therefore saw nothing new to me. But this time,—I am not thinking of St, Thomas and his doubts, either,—no sooner had I got into the church than I seemed to receive the direct permission of the Master to come. Still, I said to myself, I must not go to the communion without further refection! I must go home and duly prepare myself before I venture. But when the instant came, I found myself carried up to the altar rail, almost without my own volition. I am perfectly sure that it was right. Anyway, I could not help it.

I may mention as a reason why I do not offer to put my gratitude for the bounty granted to me into some form of church work, that that which seemed to call me today seemed to promise me that I should bear a cross like death for the Master's sake, and he would give me strength to bear it. I am sure that will happen. My part is to wait. I have never before been mystical; but now I am. After giving myself time to reflect upon the situation, I will call to see you. Yours very truly,

C. S. Peirce

It does not seem to me that it would be wise to make the circumstances known; but I conceive it my duty to report them to you. I am a man of 52, and married. (MS L483)

Peirce did not say which articles of the creed had been giving him trouble, nor had he been any more specific in the draft of a letter to the *Nation* in response to a column of 9 July 1891: "I personally am a layman who have severed my visible connection with the Church, and so put my soul in jeopardy, because I cannot believe a certain article of faith in the sense in which it is commonly understood..." (MS L159) We do however, know how he resolved this difficulty in later years: "... I say the creed in church with the rest. By doing so I only signify, as I presume the majority do,—I hope they do;—my willingness to put aside, most heartily, anything that tends to separate me from my fellow christians." (SS: 78)

The St. Thomas incident came right in the middle of the *Monist* series. It is thus not surprising that when Peirce applied his synechism to the notion of personality, he also spoke of God as person, of recognition and perception of God, and of communication with this person. But for

Peirce, a person is a sign, a general idea, and a cell within ideas of higher generality; individual personality is unimportant, nearly unreal. It is thus difficult to decide, merely on the ground that his God was personal in this sense, whether Peirce was a theist in the ordinary sense. Harrison (1971) takes Peirce to distinguish quite clearly between person-as-subject-with-potential, and actual personality or character. On the one hand, it is not clear that in the text cited by Harrison (CP 6.156-157) Peirce himself clearly made this distinction. On the other hand, a case can be made that such a distinction is faithful to his intent. It might then be applied to the case of God as follows: God and creation could be conceived as person and personality respectively. Just as in the case of a human person, personality, as its actual expression at any time, is always only a partial expression, so creation, (God's "personality," as it were) is always only a partial expression of the deity as person, that is, subject who expresses self outwardly in creation.

In addition, Peirce integrated his new concern with God as person with the earlier conception of deity as ideal end of the evolutionary process:

> ... the word coordination ... implies a teleological harmony in ideas, and in the case of personality this teleology is more than a mere purposive pursuit of a predeterminate end; it is a developmental teleology. This is personal character. A general idea, living and conscious now, it is already determinative of acts in the future to an extent of which it is not now conscious.
>
> This reference to the future is an essential element of personality. Were the ends of a person already explicit, there would be no room for development, for growth, for life; and consequently there would be no personality. The mere carrying out of predetermined purposes is mechanical ... a genuinely evolutionary philosophy, that is, one that makes the principle of growth a primordial element of the universe, is so far from being antagonistic to the idea of a personal creator that it is really inseparable from that idea .... (CP 6.156-57)

Peirce closely connected personhood and development. An already fully existent deity would not be personal. To be a person, human or divine, is to grow, both in ends and in the journey toward them. In Harrison's terms, both the person-as-subject-with-potential and the actual personality would be developmental realities.

A mechanistic approach to evolution, on the contrary, such as that of Herbert Spencer (CP 6.14), is "hostile to all hopes of personal relations to God." (MS L387a) Personal creator, personal relations: suddenly it became very important to Peirce that we be able to make person-to-person contact with God (N 1: 157), at least in the sense he gave to personality as a general idea or coordination of ideas (CP 6.155), and that we be able to recognize, or know that we know, the deity. He wondered whether his synechism might be able to explain recognition of another personality in telepathy (CP 6.159-161), but thought it might not be adequate to explain the common non-recognition of God.

> A difficulty which confronts the synechistic philosophy is this. In considering personality, that philosophy is forced to accept the doctrine of a personal God; but in considering communication, it cannot but admit that if there is a personal God, we must have a direct perception of that person and indeed be in personal communication with him. Now, if that be the case, the question arises how it is possible that the existence of this being should even have been doubted by anybody. The only answer that I can at present make is that facts that stand before our face and eyes and stare us in the face are far from being, in all cases, the ones most easily discerned. That has been remarked from time immemorial. (CP 6.162)

It is hard for me to understand why Peirce thought it odd that there should be a person with whom he had missed being in communication. In any case this passage, read after Peirce's letter to "Dear and Reverend Sir," does suggest that the existence—later the "reality"—of a personal God was now so obvious to Peirce that he wondered how he could ever have doubted it. A year later, his reply to Paul Carus's criticisms of his "The Doctrine of Necessity Examined" showed that this puzzle had continued to occupy him. Perception of the variety of the universe is a "direct, though darkling perception of God." (CP 6.613; cf. MS 958) Still,

> it does not answer the purpose to say that there is diversity because God made it so, for we cannot tell what God would do, nor penetrate his counsels. We see what He *does* do, and nothing more. For the same reason one cannot logically infer the existence of God; one can only know Him by direct perception. (CP 6.613)

In other words, although after religious experience Peirce could recognize that what he experienced was the person his synechism would lead him to hypothesize, he thought God would never appear as the conclusion of a deductive argument—later, "argumentation"—either to him or to anyone else. Although he believed he had developed the only rationally defensible philosophy in harmony with Christianity, he had "no desire to make religion a philosophical theorem; for living religion can only rest upon religious experience." (MS 961) By "living religion" he seems to have meant religion which affects the conduct of life. But such experience does constitute an argument, if not an argumentation:

> ... when a man has that experience with which religion sets out, he has as good reason—putting aside metaphysical subtleties—to

believe in the living personality of God as he has to believe in his own. Indeed, belief is a word inappropriate to such direct perception. (CP 6.436)

At about this same time Peirce began to refer often to God as a father—another way of saying that his philosophy's Absolute First might be known to religious consciousness as the "Father" of Jesus and of all believers. He asked, for example, "why observe manners toward the Heavenly Father that an earthly father would resent as priggish?" (CP 6.437) In a fragment of a draft for "Evolutionary Love," he accused the writer of the Apocalypse of having encouraged "poor ignorant Christians to believe such things of our Father, and thus sowed the seed of death and corruption in the bosom of the church!" (MS 957) Again in 1893, "How many men have said to themselves scientific experience and scientific methods make it silly to believe in anything but matter and motion,—and we must candidly acknowledge it; yet our personal religious experiences bring us into the presence of our Father and our Redeemer,—we do fervently believe that, too." (MS 866)

Peirce also associated the titles "governor of history" (CP 6.342; 5.402n2) and "governor of the universe" with the title "father" during 1892-1893. Christians, he thought, could not wish to have his promising religious philosophy stifled "by the existing scientific prejudice against first causes, or the government of the universe by a father that listens to prayer and answers it, instead of by blind and ruthless law." (MS 961; cf. N 1: 157)

What are we to make of this rather sudden turn to a traditional religious conception of God, or at least to the language in which such a conception is often expressed? In view of Peirce's use of such language to distinguish explicitly his own views from those of mechanistic necessitarianism, I do not think we can maintain that he intended, at least at this period, to keep his philosophical-scientific views in one pocket and his religion in another. Rather, he found religious experience to be one more piece of evidence—in addition to all those he had discussed in "The Doctrine of Necessity Examined"—that mechanism was incomplete even as an account of natural phenomena. Both spontaneity and teleology had to be worked in somewhere, and to this enterprise Peirce devoted his philosophical work of the early 1890s.

Nor can we assume that Peirce simply abandoned all criticism when he used religious language. This was the same Peirce who had seen in 1885 that he and Royce were simply using different words to describe the real. By God's government of the universe, for example, he probably meant God's effect on it as a final cause. What is new in these years is his comfortableness with using the traditional language at all, and his insistence that religious ideas may have pragmatic import. (CP 8: pp. 283, 285)

But unresolved tensions remain in Peirce's philosophical theology of the 1890s. God is love, that is, God is the totality of the relationships between and among human beings, but God is also father and governor. To this

New England Transcendental-Schellingian (MS 958), God's mind and human minds are continuous (CP 6.307); it is not clear whether they differ in kind or merely in degree, or just what is being said about human intelligence when we say it bears an affinity to the mind of God. But Peirce did in these years surely bring his conception of God out of the realm of purely abstract theory into the human realm where it could have some pragmatic consequences for the ordinary conduct of life (Smith, 1978: 18-22). In addition, he affirmed the necessity of religious experience—both private and communal—for the knowledge of the Absolute, and used religious experience as a kind of argument for God's reality.

1896 - 1900

A new period of Peirce's philosophical work began in 1896 and culminated in the "Vitally Important Topics" lectures of 1898, the Cambridge conferences entitled "Reasoning and the Logic of Things." These lectures, together with the work of the surrounding years, show the effects of Peirce's new respect for Plato and for Hegel, of a new attempt to formulate his categories as quality, action and law (CP 1.417-519), as well as of his efforts to work out the problems he found in the Cantorian conception of continuity (Potter and Shields, 1977). The turn of the century finds Peirce concerned with the normative sciences, and with the *summum bonum* needed to make sense of these sciences as well as of scientific inquiry in general.

The Cambridge conferences are rich sources for the study of Peirce's philosophy of religion and of his critique of theology, but this period contains little that is strikingly new in his conception of God. The insistence, not entirely ironic (Trammell, 1972), that the sacred is a matter of instinctive belief, a matter for the heart rather than for the head, merely develops his earlier reflection on religious experience. Peirce knew whereof he spoke: he thought he had himself for many years allowed his theoretical problems to confuse and mislead him. In fact, he may have allowed his philosophical difficulties to prevent the kind of direct communication the continuum hypothesis would have led him to expect (CP 6.162). In 1898 he attributed the difficulty of knowing God to confusion between instinct and reason, practice and theory, experience and reflection. He had now learned to respect the insistency of experience:

> If, walking in a garden on a dark night, you were suddenly to hear the voice of your sister crying to you to rescue her from a villain, would you stop to reason out the metaphysical question of whether it were possible for one mind to cause material waves of sound and for another mind to perceive them? If you did, the problem might probably occupy the remainder of your days. In the same way, if a man undergoes any religious experience and hears the call of his Saviour, for him to halt till he has adjusted a philosophical difficulty would

seem to be an analogous sort of thing, whether you call it stupid or whether you call it disgusting. If on the other hand, a man has had no religious experience, then any religion not an affectation is as yet impossible for him; and the only worthy course is to wait quietly till such experience comes. No amount of speculation can take the place of experience. (CP 1.655; cf. 6.493)

Peirce's God remained a person encountered and recognized in religious experience, not the conclusion of a syllogism, deductive or inductive.

Even so, Peirce continued his philosophical speculations about God's nature. It must have seemed to him likely that the Reason which functioned more and more in his cosmological speculations would turn out to correspond to the God of his religious worship. But as a scientist, as a seeker of truth, he refused to presume in advance that they would correspond, but kept this as a hope and a hypothesis, taking care not to let such speculation take the place of experience. All hypotheses are to be held lightly—this was the period of Peirce's strongest attacks on infallibilism, both theological and scientific (CP 1.148; 1.55; MS L397)—ready to be thrown out at a moment's notice when they confront the insistency of contrary experience. Again and again he identified the true philosopher as the seeker, not the teacher, of truth. Real lovers of learning and of truth—he found theologians notably deficient in the love of truth—possess both the awareness of their own ignorance which inquiry requires and the openness of heart needed to perceive and worship God. "The religious mind wants the very feeling of truth which lies at the bottom of the inquirer's heart; namely, of truth as an awful and stupendous power listening to no prayer and not to be withstood." (P 611: 110)

Peirce also continued in this period to contrast mechanistic necessitarianism with a philosophy which at least leaves room for a God (CP 1.162). Now, however, he identified the view that everything in the universe is due to the operation of blind law with a scientific infallibilism, and connected his fallibilism with his open synechistic cosmology, of which the tychism of the 1892-1893 *Monist* papers had now become only a minor aspect (CP 6.202). The fallibilist had to see the actual world—which so occupied the necessitarian—as a mere interruption of the great continuum of possibilities. This brings us to what could be considered new in the late 1890s.

Peirce's cosmological speculations of the late 1890s show how seriously he had begun to take both Plato and Hegel. From Plato he had accepted the cosmos of Ideas as the continuum of possibilities and feelings, from which the universe, by means of habit-taking, was becoming an actual specification. He would later, perhaps under the influence of Royce, see in the Platonic dialogues an early source of the *summum bonum* of concrete reasonableness he sometimes identified with God (MS 434). From Hegel he accepted the idea that evolution had its own logic, that there was a logic in things and in events to which human reasoning corresponded, or in which human reason participated. Clearly Peirce's studies of Plato and of Hegel in the 1890s contributed to the development of his conception of God.

The direction Peirce's speculations were taking under these twin influences may be discerned fairly clearly by consideration of the intertwined conceptions of creation and of the continuum as they emerge in two lectures apparently written for the 1898 Cambridge series. The first is "The Logic of Continuity" (CP 6.185-213), apparently written before James asked Peirce to "be a good boy and think a more popular plan out" (Perry, 1935, *2*: 418); the second is a study of the realism-nominalism issue (MS 439).

In "The Logic of Continuity," Peirce began by explaining that "something that is *not* a multitude of distinct individuals is *more* than every multitude of distinct individuals" (CP 6.185), whose number is indeterminate yet determinable. This he called the potential aggregate (CP 6.187), or potential collection (CP 6.186), the continuum (CP 6.188), or relational generality (CP 6.190). It seems clear that he already thought that some continua are not formed by the crowding together of individuals. In other words, he saw flaws in Cantor's set-theoretical conception of continuity. When in the 1900s he came more and more consistently to see continuity in topological, rather than in metrical, terms, he could then insist that every continuum was "more" than a collection. If then, Peirce ever identified the continuum with the mind of God, he would then have had a reason for his later insistence that a completely immanent God was impossible.

He then speculated that generally continua are derived from more general continua (CP 6.191). The continuity of the line drawn on the blackboard "is nothing but the product of the original continuity of the blackboard which makes everything upon it continuous." (CP 6.203) The existing universe is an arbitrary determination of a Platonic world of ideas (CP 6.192). "The homogeneous puts on heterogeneity." (CP 6.191) Thus we must go on to suppose an original vague chaos, from which the Platonic forms themselves are developing (CP 6.194), "by a contraction of the vagueness of that potentiality of everything in general." (CP 6.196) The qualities or forms, "relics of an ancient ruined continuum of qualities," had a being—"as real as your personal life in this minute"—similar to the "vague underexistence" (CP 6.197) in the mind of one who plans a building. In other words, the continuum from which the forms develop (CP 6.200) is the mind of God, and from this general potentiality all that is determinate and heterogeneous, whether feeling or fact, form or existence, has developed. "Those who express the idea to themselves by saying that the Divine Creator determined so and so may be incautiously clothing the idea in a *garb* that is open to criticism, but it is after all, substantially the only philosophical answer to the problem." (CP 6.199)

Here is one of Peirce's many hints that his reluctance to use religious language in philosophy was not a rejection of what he took to be the meaning of such language. Even in these lectures where he so often warned against reliance on reason when "vitally important" things were at stake, he was willing enough to draw on the resources of religious feeling to find answers to philosophical problems. The do-not-mix injunction goes only one way. No philosophy of religion can produce religion, but religious experience calls for interpretation, and thus produces philosophy of religion and philosophical theology. Peirce's later writings show even more clearly that he believed that there is *one* reality, which may be described either in the language of religion or in that of scientific philosophy. The question becomes one of appropriateness.

Peirce went on to explain that the qualitative elements in the original continuum spring up "by their own inherent firstness" and take on specificity by means of their reactions with each other:

> This reaction and this existence these persons call the mind of God. I think there is no objection to this except that it is wrapped up in figures of speech, instead of having the explicitness that we desire in science. (CP 6.199)

So the absolute chance of the original chaos of feeling has, by means of reactions, produced the evolution of forms, events, time and logic, all of which belong to the mind of God (CP 6.200). Creation is thus the process by which quality emerges into existence, existence takes on habit (CP 6.204), and thus generality. The reason inherent in, and emergent from, this process is a logic of events to which our minds aspire (CP 6.189), the mind of God. It is hardly surprising that Peirce's most laudatory comments on Hegel are found in this series of lectures.

Is the "mind of God" equivalent to the mind of nature? In the 1896 "Lessons from the History of Science," Peirce claimed that "retroduction goes upon the hope that there is sufficient affinity between the reasoner's mind and nature's to render guessing not altogether hopeless. . . ." (CP 1.121) Peirce uses "God" and "Nature" as if they were equivalent just often enough to arouse the suspicion that he sometimes thought of God in almost Spinozistic terms during this period.

A second lecture apparently intended for the Cambridge series is MS 439 on realism and nominalism. A brief examination of a few passages may throw further light on the cosmology of "The Logic of Continuity." First of all, we find the cosmos of ideas, the Platonic world, as the end as well as the beginning of evolution: God the Alpha and Omega, the double absolute of the 1880s. The geometrical mind is obedient, Peirce wrote, "to that great world-vitality which is bringing out a cosmos of ideas, which is the end toward which all the forces and all the feelings in the world are tending." (MS 439) This organized cosmos as the ideal end of things is above all Third. Thirdness is the systematic wholeness in which the world is growing—the reason in reason. And reason, according to Peirce, "is divine insofar as it fills up the gaps of the discrete and displays a continuum." (MS 438, from a fragment of "Detached Ideas," 1898)

In this lecture, the realism-nominalism question had taken on the form: are any continua real? Reality, Peirce now answered,

> ... is but a retroduction, a working hypothesis which we try, our one desperate forlorn hope of knowing anything. Again it may be, and it would seem very bold to hope for anything better, that the hypothesis of reality, though it answers pretty well, does not perfectly correspond to what is. But if there is any reality, then, so far as there is any reality, what that reality consists in is this: that there is in the being of things something which corresponds to the process of reasoning, that the world *lives,* and *moves,* and *has its being,* in a logic of events. We all think of nature as syllogising. (MS 439)

Peirce's "reality" has come to sound much like Hegel's "reason," and his obvious reference to St. Paul for whom we live, move and have our being in God (Acts 17: 28), makes it probable that Peirce meant to endow the fully real with the same religious meaning that Hegel gives to the highest and fullest development of Reason. Peirce would soon begin to speak of creation as the evolution of concrete reasonableness, the growth of reason-in-nature or God. Probably this lecture shows the direction in which his thought was moving.

Nature, Peirce continued, makes inductions and retroductions. "Evolution wherever it takes place is one vast succession of generalizations, by which matter is becoming subject to higher and higher laws; and I point to the infinite variety of nature as testifying to her Originality or power of Retroduction." (MS 439) This sounds like Nature personified; in fact it sounds like Spinoza's *natura naturans* and *natura naturata* all in one sentence. Within the same series of lectures, Peirce sounded at times more like Emerson:

> ... in all its progress, science vaguely feels that it is only learning a lesson. The value of *Facts* to *it,* lies only in this, that they belong to Nature; and Nature is something great, and beautiful, and sacred, and eternal, and real—the object of its worship and its aspiration." (CP 5.589)

Again, Peirce had no two realities, scientific and religious; the nature discovered in science *is* the sacred; religious faith required him to be a materialist "without flinching." (CP 1.354) Science is the search for the divine: "Generalization, the filling out of continuous systems, in thought, in sentiment, in deed, is the true end of life." (MS 439) Perhaps God is now final cause of generalization, first in intention and last in fulfillment.

In fact, Peirce's review of Spinoza's *Ethics* had shown a considerable appreciation for Spinoza back in 1893. Peirce criticized Spinoza's logic and his view of himself as geometer, but his religion and ethics passed the pragmatic test:

> Spinoza's ideas are eminently ideas to affect human conduct. If, in accordance with the recommendation of Jesus, we are to judge of ethical doctrines and of philosophy in general by its practical fruits, we cannot but consider Spinoza as a very weighty authority; for probably no writer of modern times has so much determined men toward an elevated mode of life. Although his doctrine contains many things which are distinctly unchristian, yet they are unchristian rather intellectually than practically. In part, at least, Spinozism is, after all, a special development of Christianity; and the practical upshot of it is decidedly more Christian than that of any current system of theology. (N 2: 86-87)

High praise this is from Peirce, and reminiscent of his discussion of Vacherot in 1878. Both thinkers are praised for the effect of their theologies upon conduct, and thus preferred to those more scrupulously orthodox. The paragraph quoted above follows Peirce's observation that Spinoza's assertions cannot be verified in the ordinary scientific manner, and seems to say here: "but this pragmatic justification is enough for me." To what extent this moral elevation inclined him to accept *Deus sive Natura,* Peirce did not tell us directly, but MS 439 may suggest that if Nature be conceived as in constant process of a teleological development toward what he began to call "concrete reasonableness," or the *summum bonum,* then this Nature may be what he was calling God.

Further support for the view that Peirce accepted an idealistic form of Spinoza's monism may be found, not only in his continuing criticism of William James's pluralism, but in his 1899 review of the *Monadology* of Leibniz.

> He is a declared nominalist, and his theory of monads breathes nominalistic individualism. But he strangely fails to see how contrary to all this is his law of continuity; and it is still more curious that he found himself at last forced to revive the substantial forms of the medieval realists. It will occur to almost every mind that for each Leibnizian monad all the rest are superfluous and non-existent—a manifest absurdity; and that so great a reasoner should not have seen the inconsistency of supposing God to be one of those monads, is quite astonishing. (N 2: 187)

Peirce thus accepted Spinoza's logic of monism, and did not, at least in the 1890s, make God something in addition to the world. Still his very work on the logic of continuity, with all its pantheistic possibilities, was probably leading him toward his transcendence affirmations of the early 1900s. In what appears to be a draft for one of the 1898 Cambridge lectures we find, "That is continuous which transcends all multitude." (MS 1109) The whole is not just the sum of the parts, but transcends it. To identify God and Nature is to say something more about the universe than simply to list the components of the world. What is this "more"? It may be the directedness of evolution toward concrete reasonableness (N 2: 208).

Clearly Peirce's thought had turned, before the end of the century, to consideration of the *summum bonum* (N 2: 220-221). This ultimate end or ideal, "neither specifically psychical nor physical" (N 2: 250), this order or rationality, is what makes other things good, useful, or reasonable, and makes sense of the evolutionary process.

"The Reasonable One"

Peirce's talk of God in the 1890s, while mainly continuous with earlier conceptions, is marked by a tone of far greater confidence than before. Theology and infallibilism are enemies both to philosophy and to religion, and speculation is not to be allowed to replace the all-important experience. The casual reader may be misled by the 1898 Cambridge conferences to think Peirce separated instinct and reason so completely as to render all reflection upon religious experience impossible. On the contrary, the 1890s show Peirce integrating such experience with his pragmatism, his evolutionary cosmology, and with his synechism. By the turn of the century, he can be seen to be nearly identifying the earlier ultimate outcome of inquiry, the truth to be discovered in the long run, with the ultimate outcome of evolution, and to be speaking of this final end, which now as *summum bonum* has normative overtones, in religious terms. Peirce's criticisms of theology, then, were surely not refusals of rational reflection on religious topics, but only of dogmatic methods and attitudes in religion.

An important feature of Peirce's work in the 1890s was his effort to replace the Cantorian, or metrical, conception of a continuum comprised of points. In addition to the mathematical difficulty that there is no greatest multitude, and thus that no multitude could add up to a continuum, Peirce found that the common sense notion of time argues against its being conceived as a succession of instants. Toward the turn of the century, he emphasized the importance of topology, as opposed to metrics, in understanding continuity (MS 948). In connection with his categories, he spoke of the generality of continuity transcending all that merely exists and reacts (MS 942). It is tempting, thus, to hypothesize that parallel with his recognition that every continuum has "something more" to it than the sum of all its points, came a belief that God, the most general of all continua, also transcends the creation which is in God. This would perhaps account for the strong transcendence-of-God affirmations of 1905. Unfortunately, I can find no evidence to support this hypothesis in the pre-1900 writings, and will thus have to look for clues to the origin of Peirce's late "theism" in the early twentieth century writings.

A related question, left unresolved by Peirce both now and in later years, is what he could possibly mean by calling God personal. If theism is belief in a personal God, then the meaning Peirce would give to "personal" is crucial for determining whether his self-designation as a "theist" was accurate. Now Emily Michael has shown clearly that the only kind of individuality Peirce admitted (CP 3.711-713) was that of a reacting Second (1976: 321-329). But this is just the kind of individuality Peirce apparently denied to God with his rejection of the question about God's existence (MS 843; CP 6.495). In fact, as my next chapter will show, Peirce tended strongly to identify God with Thirdness—with mind, continuity, generality, and resonableness. Personhood, for Peirce, meant not individuality, but generality expressed in the concrete conduct of life. Nature is the concrete expression of the mind and personhood of "the Reasonable One." (N 2: 208)

Chapter IV

THE FINAL OPINION
(1900 — 1914)

> ... to believe in reasoning about phenomena is to believe that they are governed by reason, that is, by God. (SS: 75)

Only in a thoroughly ironic sense, or in a very loose sense, can Peirce's twentieth century writings on God be considered to be a final opinion, or even *his* final opinion. The truth or reality of any matter was, for him, the opinion which the community of investigators would discover and agree upon if investigation were indefinitely prolonged. An individual's opinions, no matter what practical certainty they might have as instinctive beliefs, could thus only be provisional steps in the search for truth and in the growth of reasonableness. In addition, Peirce's last major writing on the topic of religion, his 1908 "A Neglected Argument for the Reality of God" (CP 6.452-491), repeatedly refers to God as a "hypothesis," scarcely a word to be found in creed and dogmas. God is, to be sure, an extremely attractive, almost compelling, abductive hypothesis, a vague product of the rational instinct which we cannot resist believing—today he might say a highly confirmed hypothesis—but still a hypothesis.

The task of this chapter is to discover, as much as possible, the character of Peirce's "strictly hypothetical God." Despite the idea's inevitable vagueness, Peirce thought in 1909 that it may "truly be said that each of us believes in God, and that the only quest is how to believe less crudely...." (MS 641) Peirce's writings on God after 1900 exhibit his own effort in this regard, an endeavor which required both the recognition of vagueness and the pragmatic effort to make the idea clear.

ROYCE AND PEIRCE

Considering Peirce's pronounced tendency to be critical of writings on religion, theology, and religious metaphysics, his approval of Royce's conception of God deserves notice. In his review and drafts for reviews of the two volumes of *The World and the Individual* (CP 8.100-131; MS 1461), Peirce took Royce to task for his reliance upon Hegelian logic, for his misunderstanding of realism, for his misconstrual of infinity, for his long-windedness, and for using the name of God in philosophy—"like inviting a man to see the body of his wife dissected." (CP 8.125) He qualified however: "... Things shocking to right feeling are sometimes necessary in philosophy, as they are in science." (CP 8.125) Peirce wrote to James on 12 June 1902:

> I have been studying Royce's book. The ideas are very beautiful. The logic is most execrable. I don't think it is very good taste to stuff it so full of the name of God. The Absolute is strictly speaking only God, in a Pickwickian sense, that is, in a sense that has no effect. Forgive the garrulity that comes of my eremitical life and God bless you!" (CP 8.277-278)

We may observe Peirce's two uses of "God" here. Apparently "God" is a word for use in respect to the practical upshot of theory, but not appropriate for use in theory itself. As for the "Absolute," Peirce's views fluctuated. In 1906 he wrote: "whether there be an Absolute or not, it is nothing like God." (MS 857) In any case, the "bad taste" involved in the use of the name of God in philosophy seems to be a violation of Peirce's desideratum that philosophy be a "strict science, passionless and severely fair." (CP 5.537) The "absolute," on the other hand, was not the object of religious experience or of worship.

But Royce's thought also received the closest thing to assent that Peirce ever gave to a religious philosophy. "Your statement of the relation of the individual to God is sublime and fit to satisfy the soul in life and in the hour of death. It must stand for age after age." (MS L385; cf. CP 8.117) Now of what in Royce's account did Peirce so warmly approve? Peirce provided some clues in the same letter of 28 May 1902, immediately following the passage cited above:

> My feeling is that the individual just fills his place in the revelation of the universal and except for what fragment of universal meaning he bears is of no account. Like the word "to" which fills out "Be or not be" and so helps the effect of the drama of Hamlet. If there is so much glee in heaven over one sinner that repenteth, what must be the deep ineffable felicity to Carnegie in picking up a newspaper in the elevated and so saving his copper. Individuals are cells. (MS L385)

In other words, the worth and importance of what we take to be individual life resides in the cell-like part each life plays in a larger whole which, like heaven or Carnegie's wealth, appears not to need the single individual. In truth the whole, like the esthetic whole, "To be or not to be," requires the presence of the cells. Peirce had in 1893 equated individuality with falsity, and had contrasted the "gospel of greed" with evolutionary love. He was making the same point here in 1902. Neither God nor human beings are ultimately individual.

In Volume I of *The World and the Individual,* Royce had rejected realism, mysticism, and critical rationalism as accounts of the knower-known relationship, and opted instead for his "nameless fourth conception of Being," in which the known or the thought is the purpose or plan of the knower. Peirce gave Royce credit for having broken up our mistaken tendency to think "that what one *means* to do and the meaning of a word are quite unrelated meanings of the word 'meaning'...." (CP 1.343) In fact, this was one important meaning of the 1878 pragmatic maxim (CP 5.402): words and concepts are empty without some conceivable reference to action, possible experience, and conduct. (Today we could make the same point by saying that *intension* as logical depth of meaning or connotation is not unrelated to *intention* as purpose for action.) So perhaps this fragment of universal meaning which the individual bears is partial fulfillment of the plans or purposes of God (CP 8.138n4).

In the supplementary essay to Volume 1, on "The One, the Many, and the Infinite," an essay Peirce termed "very important" (CP 8.106), Royce addressed himself to the question of the relationship between God and the human individual. Royce's problem, of course, was to show how an absolute idealism could avoid swallowing up the human individual, or, with Bradley, relegating the person to the realm of mere appearance. He had to show, contra Bradley, that the actually infinite is not a contradiction (1899: 476). He approached the problem by giving two examples of self-representative series whose infinity does not destroy the individuality of the individuals forming the series. "We want to find some case of a unity which develops its own differences out of itself." (1899: 496) Imagine a perfect map of England drawn within England. To be perfect, the map will have to contain a map of itself, which will contain a map of itself, and so on *ad infinitum*. There will be nothing contrary in conceiving the infinite number of maps as individuals, nor in seeing the whole map projection as an infinite individual.

Peirce welcomed the use of this example, amd complained only that Royce shrank from making the map-projection continuous (CP 5.71); 8.125). For Peirce the individual was a cell, only relatively independent or self sufficient (MS L385). In 1892 Peirce himself used the movement of feeling in protoplasm to illustrate his theory of continuity (CP 6.133).

The other self-representative series is that of the whole numbers (Royce, 1899: 499), a suggestion Royce said he had drawn from Cantor, from Peirce, and especially from Dedekind. Again Royce found that the actually infinite concatenated series of whole numbers contains no denial of the members of the series, and thus showed that absolute idealism need not deny the reality of the individuals which compose the infinite totality. In addition, parts of the totality may themselves be actually infinite, as in the case of the odd numbers, the powers of 2, the multiples of 5, and so on. The finite self, "the complete expression of a self-representative system of purpose and fulfillment," is, by comparsion to the Absolute Self, only partial (1901: 446). The eternal ethical individual is "infinite but partial." (1901: 447)

In terms of Royce's "fourth conception of being," the idea that every thought is a plan, and all being is the expression of purpose, we find that both the map-series and the whole-number series are orderly expressions of one original plan (1899: 509, 532). In addition, it turns out that such an actual infinite is a positive conception, and the finite is the negatively definable (1899: 511). The Absolute can now be defined as a self-representative ordered system (1899: 513-533), a true totality, given *totum simul* in the original definition of the system. The order of the system is a form of unity in multiplicity, and everything that is, "is part of a self-imaged system." (1899: 536; 553) It is not far now to Peirce in 1903: "the universe is a vast representamen, a great symbol of God's purpose, working out its conclusions in living realities." (CP 6.119)

So Royce believed himself to have shown that Reality is both determinate and individual, one and many. Both the Absolute and the individuals within it are real selves. "The Absolute is no sponge. It is not a cryptic or self-ashamed, but an absolutely self-expressive self," an "Individual of Individuals." (1899: 565; 569)

The second volume of *The World and the Individual* closes with a chapter entitled "The Union of God and Man," to which Peirce's laudatory remarks apparently refer directly. Here Royce developed what he called a theory of immortality. He admitted that from a temporal perspective much of our life seems like death, in fact, like many deaths. Works and lives and relationships seem to be prematurely cut off. From the perspective of eternity, of the Absolute Totality, however, each life and work contributes to the life and purpose of the Absolute. Indeed, if the finite individual adopts the viewpoint of the totality, it will even be seen that the deaths can only be called death in relation to some purpose which transcends, or has meaning beyond the life of, the individual. Royce here returned to his old idealistic theme: error, sin, death, and finitude all point beyond themselves toward the reality of an Absolute Mind by which, and by reference to which, they are seen as evil. In Royce's words,

> In God you possess your individuality. Your very dependence is the condition of your freedom, and your unique significance. The one lesson of our entire course has thus been the lesson of the unity of finite and infinite, of temporal dependence, and of eternal significance, of the World and all its Individuals, of the One and the Many, of God and Man. Not only in spite, then, of our finite bondage, but because of what it means and implies, we are full of the presence and the freedom of God. (1901: 417; cf. 427-429)

Small wonder that a Peirce, whose work attracted so little notice during his lifetime, should find such a conception of God consoling. But he also seems to have found it intellectually satisfying enough to continue to approve it. In MS 313, evidently a draft for the sixth of the 1903 Cambridge lectures, we find this description of the life of an evolving deity:

> A man for whom reality means much will associate it with what is most living and most intimate in experience. He will be fond of anthropomorphic conceptions of the universe. All that Professor Royce has so admirably said of the purposive element of thought as something that needs to work itself out in order to comprehend its own meaning will recommend itself to his favorable consideration. As a man upon his death-bed will review the achievements and struggles of his life as a work of art, though he did not look upon them so as he did them, as of the aesthetic quality of them as the effective sum-total of himself, so he may guess that in the long process of creation God achieves his own being.

Probably Peirce here exactly inverted Royce's conception of the Absolute Idea, which, for Royce, developed "the multitude out of the internal meaning of a single purpose" (1899: 611n2), the many from the one. Still, Peirce clearly saw his own and Royce's Absolutes as different approaches to the same conception. Royce stressed the Alpha, and Peirce the Omega.

Two years later, in a 1905 manuscript entitled "The Basis of Pragmaticism" Peirce commented that "whoever has read *The World and the Individual* will understand (despite the not unimportant logical slips of that work) that purpose is the very fatherland of evolution." (MS 283) Again we find Royce's initial creative and expressive plan conflated with Peirce's purpose, upshot, or final cause of evolution. In a 1905 draft of "The Basis of Pragmaticism," in explaining that ideas attain life only through action, Peirce wrote:

> I think Royce's conception in *The World and the Individual* (although I do not assent to the logic of that work) comes nearer to the genuine upshot of pragmaticism than any exposition that a pragmatist has given,—than any *other* pragmatist has given. (MS 284)

Here Peirce makes no direct reference to the Absolute or to God, but it will be noticed that one reason he gave in 1905 for dissociating himself from the pragmatists was their refusal to admit the Absolute. It turned out that the absolute idealist Royce was the only other philosopher who truly qualified as a pragmatist.

Finally, even the God of the religious experience in the Neglected Argument was to be understood philosophically as Royce's Absolute. As late as 22 March 1909, in a short manuscript entitled "Studies of Meaning," in which Peirce chronicled the early history of pragmatism—Metaphysical Club of 1872-1873, *Popular Science Monthly* articles of 1878, and so on—he remarked as follows:

> But some years later Professor William James brought the matter before the philosophic world (pressing it, indeed, further than Mr. Peirce, who continues to acknowledge, not the *existence,* but yet the *reality,* of the Absolute, as set forth, for example, by Royce) and in this form Pragmatism has taken a prominent place in the philosophy of today. (MS 630; cf. MS 619, 25 March 1909)

We find then that even though "my religion rather fights shy of metaphysics" (MS L385), Peirce's "strictly hypothetical God" of the Neglected Argument was still largely, on its philosophical side, Royce's Absolute. Peirce did not, in his last years, abandon philosophical thought for religious language.

1903 Harvard Lectures

But there is more to the story, and Peirce's 1902-1909 writings, though frustratingly incomplete in some cases, contain many more suggestions for philosophical theology. In the concluding section of Lecture IV of the 1903 Harvard lectures, "The Reality of Thirdness," in the context of a discussion of his theory of signs, Peirce stated his view that perceptual judgments, even of hallucinations, or so-called illusory qualities, are completely beyond our control and thus are judgments of reality, and continued:

> Therefore, if you ask me what part qualities can play in the economy of the universe, I shall reply that the universe is a vast representamen, a great symbol of God's purpose, working out its conclusions in living realities. Now, every symbol must have, organically attached to it, its Indices of Reactions and its Icons of Qualities; and such part as these reactions and these qualities play in an argument [the part of premises] that, they of course, play in the universe—that Universe being precisely an argument. (CP 5.119)

Adequate elucidation of Peirce's semiotic, or general theory of signs, would require a developmental study larger than this one, and is thus beyond the scope of this monograph. I will, however, summarize its main outlines briefly: All thought is in signs. A sign, or *representamen,* "is something which stands to somebody for something in some respect or capacity." (CP 2.228) What the sign creates in someone, the "to somebody," Peirce called its *interpretant,* itself a new sign. What is signified or represented, the "for something" of the above definition, is the sign's *object.* The idea in reference to which the sign signifies, the "in some respect," is the sign's *ground,* an "Idea," Peirce explained, "to be understood in a sort of Platonic sense." (CP 2.228) Peirce defined *sign* for Baldwin's *Dictionary of Philosophy and Psychology* (1901) as "anything which determines something else (its *interpretant*) to refer to an object to which itself refers (its *object*), in the same way, the interpretant itself becoming a sign, and so on *ad infinitum*." (CP 2.303)

Having read and approved Royce's connection of meaning and purpose as an accurate expression of pragmatism, Peirce must be saying that the object of the universe-sign is the mind or purpose of God. As the conclusion of an argument is its meaning (CP 5.175; 5.179; 5.448n1), God is what the world means: the concrete living realities, often brought about through human purpose, are the conclusion of the argument constituted by the universe, the interpretant of the universe-symbol. On the other hand, in Peirce's theory each interpretant, or mental content, becomes in turn a sign. Thus God's purpose is expressed in the universe-symbol, and continually interpreted in living realities. Now an interpretant is "something" in the interpreter (CP 8.179), something the sign creates. The universe-symbol creates the idea of esthetic totality:

> The universe as an argument is necessarily a great work of art, a great poem—for every fine argument is a poem and a symphony—just as every true poem is a sound argument. But let us compare it rather with a painting—with an impressionist seashore piece—then every Quality is one of the elementary colored particles of the Painting; they are all meant to go together to make up the intended Quality that belongs to the whole as whole. That total effect is beyond our ken; but we can appreciate in some measure the resultant Quality of parts of the whole .... (CP 5.119)

We have again God as Alpha and Omega: the originating purpose of which the universe is sign and expression, and the total outcome of "Nature's own process." In MS 7, "On the Foundations of Mathematics," (c. 1903), Peirce suggested that all signs have the same ultimate referent. Using as example the sentence "Whatever the Pope, as such, may declare will be true," he continued: "But supposing the Pope not to declare anything, does that proposition refer to any real object? Yes, to the Pope. But ... even if there were no pope, still like all other signs sufficiently complete, there is a single definite object to which it must refer; namely, to the 'True,' or the Absolute, or the entire Universe of real being...." In addition to the support it lends to this reading of 5.119—that God is the referent or object of the universe-sign—this passage explicitly identifies Truth, the Absolute, and the universe. Peirce did not object to making some things signs of themselves—the universe the sign of God. (CP 8.122n19) We may have here the "ultimate logical interpretant" of 1907 (CP 5.476). Although it may seem logically inconsistent to suggest that God and Nature are signs of each other, I suspect that Peirce could do this because he was increasingly inclined to view them as metaphysically indentifiable.

Is this "whole as whole" (CP 5.119) identical with its object, the purpose of God which the universe signifies? Peirce did not close off this possibility but 5.119 suggests that the idea of God adds to Nature whatever a stated conclusion adds to the sum of an argument's premises—esthetic wholeness. The Neglected Argument of 1908 appears in embryo here. The qualities, facts, and regularities, together with the relationships between them, begin to form a whole which suggests an extremely attractive hypothesis: God's reality.

In 1908 Peirce would be quite aware that the interpretant-God as the conclusion of the argument that is the universe must be a "strictly hypothetical God." Even earlier, in approaching the reality of God as the *summun bonum* of concrete reasonableness, however, Peirce seemed to recognize that he was using abduction: ". . . the saving truth is that there is a Thirdness in experience to which we can train our own reason to conform more and more. If this were not the case, there could be no such thing as logical goodness or badness; and therefore we need not wait until it is proved that there is a reason operative in experience to which our own can approximate" (CP 5.160).

There are also suggestions in Peirce's work at this period that the *summum bonum,* reasonable reasonableness (CP 5.121), emerges from, or is created by, the evolutionary process (CP 2.118). Nature is, he suggested in a Hegelian tone, "a gradual unfolding of thought [which] has been going on and is still going on, a process which is at once a long drawn out creation and revelation and subjugation to reason." (MS 872) Peirce concluded a draft for the first of the Lowell Lectures of 1903 with an explanation of his view—which he stated directly the same year in the "Syllabus: On Some Topics of Logic" (MS 478)—that "the process of growth is the *summum bonum.*"

> The very being of the General, of Reason, *consists* in its governing individual events. So, then, the essence of Reason is such that its being never can have been completely perfected. It always must be in a state of incipiency, of growth. It is like the character of a man which consists in the ideas that he will conceive and in the efforts that he will make, and which only develops as the occasions actually arise. Yet in all his life long no son of Adam has ever fully manifested all that was in him. So, then, the development of Reason requires as a part of it the occurrence of more individual events that ever can occur. It requires, too, all the coloring of all qualities of feeling, including pleasure in its proper place among the rest. This development of reason consists, you will observe, in embodiment, that is, in manifestation. The creation of the universe, which did not take place during a certain busy week in the year 4004 B.C., but is going on today and never will be done, is this very development of Reason. I do not see how one can have a more satisfying ideal of the admirable than the development of Reason so

understood. The one thing whose admirableness is not due to an ulterior reason is Reason itself comprehended in all its fullness, so far as we can comprehend it. Under this conception, the ideal of conduct will be to execute our little function in the operation of the creation whenever, as the slang is, it is "up to us" to do so. In logic, it will be observed that knowledge is reasonableness; and the ideal of reasoning will be to follow such methods as must develop the most speedily .... (CP 1.615)

In accord with his theory of the normative sciences, Peirce believed that, given the conception of the *summum bonum* as reasonableness, ethics depends upon esthetics—the science of the intrinsically admirable—and logic upon ethics, just as the theory predicts. (See MS L107 for more detail on Peirce's special sense of 'ethics' and 'esthetics'.) But for the purposes of this study, the interest in this passage lies mainly in the triple use of the expression "the development of Reason." The ambiguous phrase "of Reason" has an objective or a subjective genitive. It leaves open, probably intentionally, the possibility that Reason is already there and then develops by self-expression and manifestation, and the alternative possibility that Reason is the ideal final result of evolution. In this passage both meanings seem to be intended. The *summum bonum* is already and not yet, Alpha and Omega, perhaps like every final cause, first in intention and last in fulfillment. Peirce seems to have held from the 1880s onward that creation is a chaos-becoming-cosmos process. Potential order becomes actual order. And as Royce had pointed out, everything real shares the purposeful, already and not-yet, character of ideas. Pragmaticism, Peirce would say in 1905 with the same perhaps deliberate ambiguity, "makes the development of the idea alone the *summum bonum*." (MS 284)

Peirce's published writings at this period tend to speak less of God than of the *summum bonum*, of "reasonableness" or Reason, and of the Absolute, but we must remember that he had only accused the God-talking Royce of philosophical bad taste, not of being mistaken. On 14 July 1905 Peirce wrote to Francis C. Russell:

Your *summum bonum*, 'life' is probably about the same as mine, though I view it more concretely. I look upon creation as going on and I believe that such vague idea as we can have of the power of creation is best identified with the idea of theism. So then the ideal would be to be fulfilling our appropriate office in the work of creation. Or to come down to the practical, every man sees some task cut out for him. Let him do it, and feel that he is doing what God made him in order that he should do. (CP 8.138n4)

When we do our part in promoting reasonableness, we not only express and fulfill the purpose of God, as Royce had claimed, but we also promote the growth, or coming into being, of God. Although Peirce later hesitated to attribute growth to God, his identification of God with an evolutionary *summum bonum* forced him to admit that God grows—achieves being. (MS 313; CP 6.466) He identified the deity of theistic religions with the reasonableness aspect of all evolutionary growth and process.

God as *summum bonum* emerges from the growth of reasonableness, or more accurately, *is* that growth. Moreover, the world grows as the expression of God's mind. The laws of nature are God's ideas. (CP 1.239) In the fourth of the 1903 Cambridge lectures, "The Reality of Thirdness," speaking of generality, he suggested:

> ... that the laws of nature are ideas or resolutions in the mind of some vast consciousness, who, whether supreme or subordinate, is a Deity relatively to us. I do not approve of mixing Religion and philosophy; but as a purely philosophical hypothesis, that has the advantage of being supported by analogy. Yet I cannot clearly see that beyond that support to the imagination it is of any particular scientific service.... (CP 5.107)

The process of evolution consists in the fulfillment of these ideas, resolutions, or purposes of the deity's mind. Taken together with the accounts of creation as a process of chance working in the chaos to produce habit and order, this passage makes Peirce's cosmology sound much like Plato's in the *Timaeus*. Not necessarily a "Supreme Being" but a "Deity relatively to us," is the *Demiourgos* working to bring order into the chaos of necessity by means of ideas. In both cases the cosmos intended is the best possible, and expresses a purpose: the growth of order or reasonableness. Also in both cases the function of chance is difficult to determine, but clearly involved. In Plato, the errant cause seems to be belong to the chaos, and to be one more element of the necessity which reason must persuade. For Peirce, chance is that factor in creation which loosens the bonds of necessity, to use a Jamesian phrase, enough that growth can take place. To support this comparison, we find among the manuscripts MS 434 from 1902, in which for 234 pages Peirce traced the conception of the *summum bonum* through Plato's dialogues. At the very least we know that Peirce was deeply interested in Plato during this period.

Still, it would be misleading to leave the impression that Peirce's deity was no more than a version of Plato's Demiurge. The Demiurge seems never to be an object of religion for Plato, while Peirce's God, whether as source of reasonableness in nature, or as that reasonableness itself, is beautiful, admirable and worthy of reverence. (CP 5.589) In addition, Peirce's most common argument for a God was from human mind to divine creative reasonableness in which we must somehow share. "To believe in a god at all, is not that to believe that man's reason is allied to the originating principle of the universe?" he asked in the first chapter of the 1902 "Minute Logic."

(CP 2.24) A few pages later he answered:

> These tendencies [to generalized explanation] are irrepressible: in the long run they will cause that which they need to come into being. But much more than that, they are thoroughly reasonable; and that which they call for ought to be. Now that which they demand above all is the fact and the admission that the world is reasonable—reasonably susceptible to becoming reasonable—or in other words, that man is made after his maker's image. (CP 2.34)

Again a process-God is suggested. To be reasonable is to have a tendency to become reasonable, and it is precisely in such reasonableness that the resemblance of our minds to God's mind consists. Whether, for the purpose of a specific discussion, he considered God as beginning or as end, Peirce's thought led toward a conception of God (or Reason) becoming God (or reasonableness): "... the essence of Reason is such that its being can never have been completely perfected. It must always be in a stage of incipiency, or growth ...." (CP 1.615) And again, "the process of growth is the *summum bonum*." (MS 478) Now this Reason or reasonableness manifests itself in the growth of the laws of nature, which—as Peirce wrote to Langley, in a footnote to his 1901 manuscript on Hume and the laws of nature—themselves support belief in an intelligent creative mind which energizes itself in the world:

> Generality, as commonly understood, is not the whole of my "reasonableness." It includes *Continuity,* of which, indeed, Generality is but a cruder form. Nor is this all. We refuse to call a design reasonable unless it be feasible. There are certain ideas which have a character which our reason can in some measure appreciate but which it by no means creates, which character insures their sooner or later getting realized. What machinery may be requisite for this I do not ask. But the laws of nature have, I suppose, been brought about in some way; and so, it would seem that they were of such a nature as inevitably to realize themselves. These, then are the naked abstract characters that must be recognized in the "reasonableness" of a law of nature. Whether or no it be a legitimate presumption from those characters that nature has an intelligent author, I certainly do not see how the abstractions could, better than in that statement, be clothed in the concrete forms which many minds require, or how they could better be connected with appropriate sentiments. (Wiener, 1958: 301n45)

Several points are of interest here. First, Peirce's "reasonableness" cannot be a completely settled state of affairs even as the ideal outcome of evolution. It is inherently active, creative, energizing in the world. Reasonableness, paradoxically, has the dual function of settling things—beliefs, habits, laws of nature—and of unsettling them. Both functions are, for Peirce, creative. In addition, reasonableness always exhibits the tendency toward generality. Individual qualities or facts, and even the comparisons between things, are not reasonable; general characters which form behavior, ideas which are feasible, are. Though generality, even as purpose, is not the whole of reasonableness, it is a necessary condition of the reasonable.

Reasonableness also includes continuity. (Wiener, 1958: 301n45) Peirce's "the sole Ancient of Days is Continuity in the abstract..." (NEM 4: xxiv) did not always represent his thinking; here he seemed to say that continuity needs a dose of pragmatic feasibility to make it identifiable with reasonableness. His occasional use of the expression "concrete reasonableness" (CP 5.3) suggests this practical element.

Finally, he suggested that the concrete form of the abstraction "reasonableness" is the "presumption that nature has an intelligent author." So the laws of nature themselves, even apart from the scientific research which discovers them, constitute an argument—"any process of thought reasonably tending to produce a definite belief" (CP 6.456)—in a creator which in a concrete religious context would be called God. In writing to Lady Welby, Peirce explained, "... to believe in reasoning about phenomena is to believe that they are governed by reason, that is, by God." (SS 75)

Now to make such a claim surely confronts the optimistic Peirce with the problem of evil, a problem which he treated in 1903 in the customary idealistic manner by inviting the sufferer to take a larger perspective:

> My taste must doubtless be excessively crude, because I have no esthetic education; but as I am at present advised the aesthetic Quality appears to me to be the total unanalizable impression of a reasonableness that has expressed itself in a creation. It is a pure Feeling, but a feeling that is the impress of a Reasonableness that Creates. It is the Firstness that truly belongs to a Thirdness in its achievement of a Secondness. As a matter of opinion, I believe that Glory shines out in everything like the sun and that any aesthetic odiousness is merely our Unfeelingness resulting from obscurations due to our own moral and intellectual aberrations. (MS 310)

This passage confirms the impression that the deity is the reasonable aspect of the whole evolutionary process, and is involved in all three categories. To see the universe esthetically, however, is to focus on its Thirdness. Pain, as Peirce would say later, is a First, and thus neither good nor evil (MS 649); to apprehend its goodness in the esthetic whole is to see it as "Firstness that truly belongs to a Thirdness in its achievement of a Secondness." Suffice it to say, Peirce did not think that evil confronted his religious belief with any serious problem. It is all a matter of learning to discern (CP 6.162)—something Peirce would try to teach in the "Neglected Argument" of 1908.

Anthropomorphism and Theism

Meanwhile, there were a few more developments. In 1903 Peirce began to speak frequently of "anthropomorphism" in respect to the universe and to God, a way of speaking he retained through 1906. This anthropomorphism might be seen as a return to his youthful ways of speaking (MS 891) after years of writing in more abstract terms. But Peirce, usually so ready to recount his own intellectual history, did not enlighten us on this point. Nor, however, did he introduce his "anthropomorphism" as a new development in his thinking. It thus seems best to construe it as another of his "or" locutions, another way to talk about the reasonableness of the universe, and as an expression of what he began toward the middle of the decade to call his "critical commonsensism."

The earliest clear statements of what Peirce called "anthropomorphism" are to be found in the Cambridge lectures on pragmatism (1903); in fact, most of his references to it appear in these lectures. Peirce was generally most likely to call himself an "anthropomorphist" when he wanted to distinguish himself from other pragmatists who, he thought, carried empiricism too far, especially in their denial of the Absolute. Perhaps the most complete 1903 account appears, however, in Peirce's review of Baldwin's *Dictionary of Philosophy and Psychology* for the *Nation:*

> To the same general [anti-agnostic] tendency belongs an opinion, now very common, that it is unscientific to inquire whether there be a God; the only rational question being what sort of God there is. With this is naturally associated the further opinion that instead of its being shallow philosophy to suppose an "anthropomorphic" God, if by "anthropomorphic" be meant *mental,* it is far more consonant with the method of science to formulate the problem by asking what sort of a mind God is; and if we cannot understand God's mind, all science, it is said with some color of justice, must be a delusion and a snare. (CP 8.168)

It is true that Peirce did not claim here that this was his own opinion, but there is plenty of contemporaneous evidence to show that it was. It turns out that this anthropomorphism is mainly a tag Peirce used for his view that the universe is reasonable. For instance, in a fragment of Lecture IV of the 1903 Cambridge lectures, Peirce claimed that

> ... every scientific explanation of a natural phenomenon is a hypothesis that there is something in nature to which the human reason is analogous; and that it really is so all the successes of science in its applications to human convenience are witnesses. They proclaim that truth over the length and breadth of the modern world. In the light of the successes of science there is a degree of baseness in denying our

birthright as children of God and shamefacedly slinking away from anthropomorphic conceptions of the universe. (CP 1.316; also 5.47; MS 313)

Peirce's anthropomorphism expressed his metaphysical idealism. Any reality is at bottom psychical. "The one intelligible theory of the universe is," Peirce believed, "that matter is effete mind." (CP 6.25) To say something about reality as a whole, therefore, is to describe it in mental, or anthropomorphic, terms. Peirce's studies of the history and methods of science made him think this conclusion unavoidable. He also hinted in 1904 that anthropomorphism followed from pragmatism, but did not elaborate. (CP 8.191) To attribute "effete mind" to all reality was to make everything purposeful—surely both pragmatic and anthropomorphic.

The references to an anthropomorphic God continued into 1905 and 1906, and form a major part of Peirce's effort to distinguish his "pragmaticist" views from those of other pragmatists. In 1905 he claimed not to understand the humanism of the English pragmatist F. C. S. Schiller (Scott, 1973; cf. MS 331), but to "heartily embrace most of the clauses" of anthropomorphism:

> ... I do not believe that man can have the idea of any cause or agency so stupendous that there is any more adequate way of conceiving it than as vaguely like a man. Therefore, whoever cannot look at the starry heaven without thinking that all this universe must have had an adequate cause, can in my opinion not otherwise think of that cause half so justly than by thinking it is God. (CP 5.536; cf. MS L387; Potter, 1973)

The formulation is changed here, from mind to agency, but probably this is merely a change of emphasis; for a pragmaticist "mind" and "active purpose" are equivalent expressions. The context had also changed. Peirce was using his critical common-sensism, and his theory of vague instinctive beliefs (which become controversial the moment we attempt to make them precise) to explain just where his disagreement with the pragmatists lay. (MS 318) In his 1905 manuscript entitled "The Basis of Pragmaticism" he opined that many people reject pragmaticism because they have

> ... failed to perceive that it does not necessarily carry with it various other doctrines which have been associated with it and to which I am as adverse as they are. The chief of these is the entire denial of the Absolute, the setting up of a finite god or gods if any governor of the universe .... I think my fellow pragmatists are so fond of clear thinking that they insist that every concept they entertain should be definite, though clearness and definiteness are quite different things .... (MS 284)

So Peirce would give his conception of God as much pragmatic clarity as possible—he had always been willing to evaluate concepts of God in terms of their effects upon the conduct of life—but would not claim for it definiteness and precision. He continued,

> For my part, I should fear to be misunderstood if I said I believed in the Absolute, but I am one of those who say, "we believe in one God, the Father Almighty, maker of heaven and earth, and of all things visible and *invisible*," where the invisible things, I take it, are Love, Beauty, Truth, the Principle of Contradiction, Time, etc. Clearly I can have but the vaguest analogical notion of the Maker of such things, and Pragmatism, I am sure, does not require that all my beliefs should be definite. (MS 284)

The vague was for Peirce an important logical notion. In fact, he insisted, we must admit that there are "real vagues," as well as real possibilities. (CP 5.453) Vagueness is not ambiguity, to be resolved by a simple distinction; it is real indefiniteness, characterizing ideals, generals, the not yet fully accomplished Omega. Nor is vagueness equivalent to lack of meaning; the vague has pragmatic meaning in its influence upon conduct.

In addition, it seems clear from a series of letters and drafts of letters to William James in July 1905, that it was Peirce's "anthropomorphism" which became his "theism." It was in this correspondence, and in his letter to Francis C. Russell quoted above, that Peirce most clearly and repeatedly characterized himself as a theist, and from this correpondence it is possible to gain some sense, both positive and negative, of what he meant. Peirce had expected to teach a week of logic in summer school and had just found out, to his deep disappointment, that he would not get the chance (Perry, 1935, 2: 434-35). He wrote to James on 22 July 1905:

> My only comfort is in religion. I *am* a theist,—not a pagan like you. It is a religion, paganism, but to my mind little better than none. This finite god of yours must have rivals no doubt. Existence consists in reaction. It must be a whole genus. And they have, I suppose, no religion at all. They are wretched atheists with no ideals. The true theist's God is a being whom we can only vaguely know; but his essence is reality. The Idea—He *Is*. When we attempt to think out what He is, we fall into contradictions because he is above human comprehension. That is what we *all* love and adore, and this loving adoration is the best proof of His *Being,* which is not *existence* but creation. Your finite gods may be very respectable but they are creatures to criticize. The true Ideal is the living Power.... To think of the true theist's God is balm to the Heart. It comforts one for one's own shortcomings.... (MS L224)

This letter contains many elements of Peirce's mature "theism"—the version he apparently held from then on. On the issue of God's infinity he agreed with Royce rather than with James. Only a deity who is *one* could make of the universe a coherent whole, and only an infinite God could be one.

Closely related to the question of infinity was that of reality and existence. God does not exist; to say so would be fetishism (CP 6.495), making God a mere thing, another item in the universe reacting as a Second with all the other items. To say God exists is to opt for James's finite god, "one of a genus," at best a polytheism. "Existence is reaction, and therefore no existent can be *clear supreme*." (CP 8.262)

Reality, on the other hand, has no such negative implications. "I define the *real* as that which holds its character on such a tenure that it makes not the slightest difference what any man or men may have *thought* them to be, or ever will have *thought* them to be . . . but the real thing's character will remain absolutely untouched." (CP 6.495, ca. 1906) God's reality is both creation, more as process than as product, and esthetic ideal. Ideals, Peirce was convinced, are the most real of all realities. (SS 23) "The true Ideal is the Living Power." (MS L224) To suppose the ultimate ideal to be unreal would be to make nonsense of all inquiry: Peirce's version of the ontological argument. "His essence is reality." (MS L224) In other words, a pragmatic sort of reality is inclined within the ideal of the *summum bonum*. Without such reality, the ideal would be pragmatically empty.

But this infinite reality, though known directly by instinct and only vaguely by thought, was, for Peirce, no abstract empty concept reached by negative theologizing. (CP 6.502) We do know something of creation—and thus of the creator—through science, and something of the living power of ideals. This positive, though still vague, conception of the theistic God emerges more clearly in two more drafts of this same letter to James, the first dated 23 July 1905, the second 26 July:

> . . . anthropomorphism for me implies above all that the true Ideal is a living power, which is a variation of the ontological proof. . . . That is, the aesthetic ideal, that which we *all* love and adore, the altogether admirable, has as *ideal,* necessarily a mode of being to be called living. Because our ideas of the infinite are extremely vague and become contradictory the moment we attempt to make them precise. But still they are not utterly unmeaning, though they can only be interpreted in our religious adoration and the consequent effects upon conduct. This I think is good sound solid strong pragmatism. (CP 8.262)

> . . . it is impossible to think that the ideal of our hearts is merely existent or limited another way, and it is impossible for a person who puts metaphysical definitions aside to think that the object of one's love is not living. The idea is a vague one, but it is only the more irresistable

for that.... If I had the opportunity to inculcate my logic, the secret of which is to view it as semiotic (thus leading at once to immediate perception) perhaps there might have been students of sufficient voice to give weight to esthetic theism. (MS 1224)

Thus we know God positively, though not precisely. We can know the esthetic ideal as a living power. The *summum bonum* has become more than the ideal outcome of inquiry and evolution; it is the living power of beauty to attract us irresistibly. The pragmatist sees this power interpreted in worship, in human conduct, and in the "filiation" of the human heart and mind to God. "Vaguely like a man" must then mean God is somehow mind and heart, cognitivity and affectivity.

Though for this study, as for Peirce's immediate purposes in these letters, the instinct-reason question is not central, the critical common-sensist's view that some beliefs are indubitable and irresistible reinforces the impression that Peirce's deity is no conclusion to a deductive argument. "God" is a living being, a hypothesis vaguely yet powerfully suggested by the beauty and lovableness of the universe continually being created (CP 6.505). This view Peirce labelled "esthetic theism," probably an appropriate tag for his religious views to the end of his life.

The final sentence of the third draft quoted from the letter to James contains a suggestion that this "esthetic theism" would be the outcome of a sufficiently developed logic viewed as semiotic, or sign-theory. This seems consistent with the view he had expressed in 1903 that the universe is a vast symbol of God's purpose being worked out in creation (CP 5.119). A well-developed instinct for interpretation would provide the "immediate perception" Peirce had been missing in 1892 (CP 6.162). How to acquire this skill at immediate perception, at reading the signs which the universe provides, is the lesson of the 1908 "Neglected Argument."

Meanwhile, in the *Collected Papers,* there is a manuscript entitled "Answers to Questions concerning my Belief in God" (CP 6.494-521, 1905; cf. MS 861), in which are raised many traditional questions of natural theology. On several questions—whether God is omniscient, omnipotent, infallible—Peirce took an agnostic position. Yes, in a vague sense, but "we only wildly gabble about such things." (CP 6.509) In fact Peirce took a strong position here for the vagueness of all religious language and assertion (CP 5.494), to which the principle of non-contradiction is not applicable. (Potter, 1976: 235-36) But this vagueness does not deprive the objects of these signs of reality (CP 5.453); nor does it rob them of pragmatic import, the third degree of clearness. The vagueness is like the indefiniteness of the "some" in "Some side of the die will come up": it has meaning, but not precisely assignable meaning. This indefiniteness results at least partly from the reference to the future. Vagueness does not mean just that exact meaning has *not yet* been assigned, but rather that an attempt to precide would destroy the truth of the statement. The attempt to precide is especially futile in the case of the deity:

> *Questioner D:* But am I to be told that I mean nothing by God but the Creator? *Pragmaticist:* No, I do not say that. The concept of God,—if concept be the word,—is necessarily vague in the extreme. Unless, like some pragmatists, we are to satisfy ourselves with a finite God, as I emphatically cannot, or with some other low and unworthy conception, we cannot avoid contradictions. I do not see that we can mean anything by the *being* of God, but a being that is indefinite. But in those respects in which a concept is vague and therefore liable to be contradictory, it plainly cannot be a pragmaticistic meaning, and therefore should not be considered as intellectual. Possibly it would do to say that it is a rational emotion; but it really seems to belong to no recognized type of representation. If I say "some man can lift a ton," I cannot say the word "some" has no meaning in my mind, but I am at a loss to characterize that meaning. (MS 288, 27 April 1905; cf. CP 8.138n4 and MS 289, c. 1905)

Peirce here seems to oppose vagueness not only to definiteness but also to pragmatic clarity. He leaves open the possibility, however, that vague beliefs can influence our conduct in those respects in which they are clear. Belief in the order of nature, for example, leads scientists to investigate; belief in a deity, Peirce would hold in 1908, has a "commanding influence over the whole conduct of life of its believers." (CP 6.490) Still, the essential vagueness of such beliefs makes futile and misleading all attempts—by theologians, for example—to make them definite. The danger "does not lie in believing too little but in believing too much." (CP 5.517)

According to the critical common-sensist, these vague beliefs—in God or in the order of nature—rest on instinct, and the instinct of the pragmatist can be prepared by meditation.

> Let a man drink in such thoughts as come to him in contemplating the psycho-physical universe without any special purpose of his own; especially the universe of mind which coincides with the universe of matter. The idea of there being a God over it all will of course often be suggested; and the more he considers it, the more he will be enwrapt with Love of this idea. He will ask himself whether or not there really is a God. If he allows instinct to speak, and searches his own heart, he will at length find that he cannot help believing it . . . . (CP 6.501)

Soon Peirce would call this process "musement," and recognize it as an argument, illustrative of the logic of hypothesis. Meanwhile he asked how the pragmatist would conceive this God. His answer again suggested a God/Nature equivalence:

... just as long acquaintance with a man of great character may deeply influence one's whole manner of conduct ... just as the study of the works of Aristotle may make him an acquaintance, so if contemplation of the physico-psychical universe can imbue a man with principles of conduct analogous to the influence of a great man's works or conversation, then that analogue of a mind—for it is impossible to say that *any* human attribute is literally applicable—is what he means by "God". . . . the discoveries of science, their enabling us to *predict* what will be the course of nature, is proof conclusive that, though we cannot think any thought of God's we can catch a fragment of His thought, as it were. (CP 6.502)

The pragmaticist then will consider the question of God's reality equivalent to the question whether all science is an arbitrary figment, whether (for example) Buddha, Confucius, Jesus, and Socrates, all of whom meditated on nature, had their conduct modified by truth or by mere arbitrariness. this will be the question "whether the super-human courage which such contemplation has conferred upon priests who go to pass their lives with lepers and refuse all offers of rescue is merely silly fanaticism, the passion of a baby, or whether it is strength derived from the power of the truth." (CP 6.503) Only the hypothesis of God's reality, known through the physical-psychical universe, can, for the pragmaticist, make sense of science, of great spiritual leaders, and of religious heroism.

Peirce's view here resembles that of his father who believed, with the Puritans, that science is the study of God's works. (Murphey, 1961: 13) In a short 1906 manuscript entitled "Pragmatism Made Easy," Peirce reflected that "I must count it as one of the most fortunate circumstances of a life which the study of scientific philosophy in a religious spirit has steeped in its joy, that I was able to know something of the inwardness of the early growth of several of the great ideas of the Nineteenth Century . . . ." (MS 325; cf. CP 1.127) Peirce also continued to see creative activity "as an inseparable attribute of God" (CP 6.506). God is not so much the past, but rather the present, creator of the universe (CP 6.505), and in regard to us, "God is perpetually creating us, that is developing our real manhood, or spiritual reality. Like a good teacher, he is engaged in detaching us from a false dependence on him." (CP 6.507; cf. 5.402n3) Prayer is our expression of our consciousness of our relation to God, "which is nothing more than precisely the pragmatistic meaning of the name of God." (CP 6.516) This kind of prayer, calling on the name of God, is efficacious and creative of "spiritual good and moral strength." (CP 6.156) Peirce regarded his views on creation as having long been consistent, and referred back to the *Monist* articles of 1892-1893.

1908 - 1914

Among Peirce's last published writings, and surely his most famous on religious topics, is the 1908 *Hibbert Journal* article "A Neglected Argument for the Reality of God" (CP 6.452-485) with its 1910 "Additament." (CP 6.486-491) Its major concern was to outline a method by which religious experience, and thus religious belief, could become available to everyone, and to show how this process illustrates the very logic of science Peirce had spent much of his life developing. The hypothesis of God's reality, generated in the free play of musement (cf. SS: 77), has its pragmatic consequences made explicit by deduction, and its expected effects on the conduct of life—conduct in a very broad sense—checked by induction. Peirce's many affirmations of his belief in the affinity of God with the reasonableness of nature could scarcely be more dramatically expressed. To reason scientifically is to discover this reasonableness, and presupposes at least an implicit belief in God. Although at first glance it might seem odd that Peirce chose a religious topic to illustrate his logic of science, he seems to have thought the example excellent.

Since this article has been well-discussed elsewhere (Trammell, 1972; Clarke, 1977), especially with respect to Peirce's instinct-reason distinction, I will restrict my treatment to three topics which bear directly on his conception of God. Two, growth and the esthetic, are familiar by now; one is new: God as *ens necessarium*.

Growth, which Peirce had long viewed as indicative of a creative element in the universe (MS 674), and as the best evidence that the necessitarians were mistaken, now plays a central role throughout this article. It first appears as an example of the Third Universe of experience, the categories of signs whose being consists in the power to make connections. (CP 6.455) Next, we are told that the conclusion of his argument will appear, not as a theological proposition, "but in a form directly applicable to the conduct of life, and full of nutrition for man's highest growth." (CP 6.457) In the musement process itself, the occurrence of growth within and among the three universes, with its "provision for later stages in earlier ones... is a specimen of certain lines of reflection which will inevitably suggest the hypothesis of God's Reality." (CP 6.465)

So pervasive is this growth feature of all reality that, reluctantly, the believers must even ask whether God grows. The very hypothesis of God's reality is vague yet true in proportion to its growth definiteness.

> The hypothesis being thus itself subject to the law of growth, appears in its vagueness to represent God as so, albeit this is directly contradicted in the hypothesis from its very first phase. But this apparent attribution of growth to God, since it is ineradicable from the hypothesis, cannot, according to the hypothesis, be flatly false. Its implications concerning the Universes will be maintained in the hypothesis, while its implications concerning God will be partly

> disavowed, and yet held to be less false than their denial would be. Thus the hypothesis will lead to our thinking of the features of each Universe as purposed; and this will stand or fall with the hypothesis. Yet a purpose essentially involves growth, and so cannot be attributed to God. Still it will, according to the hypothesis, be less false to speak so than to represent God as purposeless. (CP 6.466; cf. 6.157)

If growth is the principal surprising fact which leads to the formation of the hypothesis of God's reality, and human self-controlled growth in conduct of life (CP 6.480) is the best inductive evidence for its truth, then unwelcome as the conclusion may be, growth must somehow be admitted as part of God's nature. With his creation cosmology of emerging reasonableness, Peirce can surely accomodate such a result. The universe, and people in it, grow reasonable by means of habit taking. The esthetic ideal grows by means of being expressed. "In the long process of creation God achieves his own being." (MS 313)

In the *Hibbert Journal* article we see that Peirce's attention to the normative sciences, especially to esthetics, bears fruit. The pure play of the esthetic experience of beauty is central to the musement process which leads to the hypothesis of God's reality (CP 6.458; 461). In addition, many of musement's objects are the beauties of nature (CP 6.462). "Why should sunsets have the exquisite poeticalness that they have? Why should all the flowers and butterflies have their different kinds of beauty?" (MS 843) Above all, when the hypothesis actually presents itself to the muser, "the more he ponders it, the more it will find response in every part of his mind, for its beauty, for its supplying an ideal of life...." (CP 6.465) Anyone who considers the universe in the light of this hypothesis

> in scientific singleness of heart, will come to be stirred to the depths of his nature by the beauty of the idea and by its august practicality, even to the point of earnestly loving and adoring his strictly hypothetical God, and to that of desiring above all things to shape the whole conduct of life and all the springs of action into conformity with that hypothesis. (CP 6.467)

Thus Peirce's "esthetic theism" is concrete and full of pragmatic import.

The most ambiguous, and the newest, feature of Peirce's theism to appear in the "Neglected Argument" is his characterization of God as *ens necessarium*. Peirce was familiar with Anselm's ontological argument which required the existence of God in order to think the concept of God, and indeed, Peirce himself used a variation of this argument from at least 1905 on. In fact, the Neglected Argument itself—not the "Humble Argument" which more closely resembles the argument from design—may be seen as a version of this proof. In addition, Peirce knew the work of Thomas Aquinas (MS 683; 1913), and could scarcely have used the expression "ens necessarium" without thinking of the "third way" of the *Summa Theologiae* (1a, qu. 2, art. 3), the argument from the being of contingent beings to that of a necessary one. So Peirce clearly wanted to indicate that the deity to which the three-ply argument would lead was at least closely related to that of medieval Christian theology. (The additament of 1910 explains that the *Hibbert Journal* article had sketched a nest of three arguments: 1. the results of musement, or the "humble argument" (CP 6.486); 2. a "neglected" theological reflection showing that the humble argument led to the idea of God (CP 6.487); and 3. the situation of this "humble argument" in the logic of science: retroduction, deduction, induction.)

Not surprisingly, however, Peirce brought his own theoretical resources to bear again on the question of how God is to be conceived. The term *Ens necessarium* is introduced in the very first sentence: "God" is "*the* definable proper name, signifying *Ens necessarium;* in my belief Really creator of all three Universes of Experience." (CP 6.452; cf. MS 843) We are told nothing about the meaning of the expression, but note that even in such a brief statement, Peirce found it important to mention that God is also creator.

The first explanation follows immediately upon the "argument from growth" considered above:

> It is not that such phenomena [of growth] might not be capable of being accounted for, in one sense, by the action of chance with the smallest conceivable dose of a higher element; for if by God be meant the *Ens necessarium,* that very hypothesis [of God's reality] requires that such should be the case. But the point is that that sort of explanation leaves a mental explanation just as needful as before. Tell me, upon sufficient authority, that all cerebration depends upon movements of neurites that strictly obey certain physical laws, and that thus all expressions of thought, both external and internal, receive a physical explanation, and I shall be ready to believe you. But if you go on to say that this explodes the theory that my neighbor and myself are governed by reason, and are thinking beings, I must frankly say that it will not give me a high opinion of your intelligence. (CP 6.465)

I take Peirce to be saying here, at the very least, that *Ens necessarium* is the God of philosophers and scientists, who also needs to be understood religiously as an adorable and lovable creator, that the language of scientific philosophy does not eliminate the need for religious language, and that the two languages are reciprocally translatable.

In the 1910 "Additament," Peirce directly addressed the pragmatic meaning of *Ens necessarium,* a vague, obscure, explanatory hypothesis of a disembodied spirit. (CP 6.489) *Ens necessarium,* Peirce suggested, is a tendency toward generalization of order, "Super-order," uniformity, "that of which order and uniformity are particular varieties." (CP 6.490) This orderliness or mind manifests itself in the capacity and tendency of things to take habits. Again it seems that the organic metaphor of growth—from chaos to cosmos—is at the very heart of Peirce's argument.

In a passage which invites comparison with the "third way" of Aquinas (1964: qu. 2, art. 3), Peirce explained that any matter-of-fact requires some super-order. (CP 6.490; MS 843) The emergence of anything from the chaos of pure possibility would require the *Ens necessarium*. General laws, and the predictability they bring, are the pragmatic meaning, or intellectual import, of the expression. *Ens necessarium* is thus another way of expressing the growth of the universe toward reasonableness, and is another of Peirce's inclusive "or" locutions. It again expresses the view that if the universe is intelligible, as science assumes it to be, it must be necessary, exhibiting generality, and its source must be necessary reasonableness. So to give the pragmatic meaning of *Ens necessarium* is to situate it within the conceptual framework of Peirce's whole cosmology. It is true that Peirce noted as the third peculiarity of this explanatory hypothesis that it exerts a "commanding influence over the whole conduct of life of its believers." (CP 6.490) But he did not spell this out; what he did explain at length was the conceptual import of *Ens necessarium*. (CP 6.491)

Another notable feature of Peirce's late "theism" was his rejection of a merely immanent God. In about 1907 he tells us that Peircean humanism would be interested in "One Incomprehensible but Personal God, not immanent in but creating the universe." (CP 5.496; cf. MS 861) In 1907, in a draft for the "Neglected Argument," he defined: "I do *not* mean by God a being merely 'immanent in nature', but I mean that being who has created every content of the world of ideal possibilities, of the world of physical facts, and the world of all minds, without any exception whatever." (MS 843) Finally, in the published version of the "Neglected Argument" we find the argument described as "that course of meditation upon the three Universes which gives birth to the hypothesis and ultimately to the belief that they, or at any rate two of the three, have a Creator independent of them . . . ." (CP 6.483) The notable commonality of these passages is their clear contrasting of immanence not with transcendence but with creative activity. Peirce's final view of creation was not merely that of a Plotinian emanation, but something more like the view of Henry James, Sr., that God creates in order to have something to love. But how is this something *other*? Perhaps there is a clue in Peirce's hesitation as to whether God is independent creator of two, or of all three, universes. Because Peirce so often identified God with Intelligence, Reason, and Mind, I assume that he was sure that God is at least partially other than the worlds of ideal possibilities and physical facts. Now ideal possibilities and brute facts, Firsts and Seconds, could, for Peirce, only incompletely account for experience, so could surely not be identical with God. (MS 843) Even the world of finite minds would require an infinite mind as its source. Only the ideal wholeness of Reason could be fully real, and thus a transcendent creator.

Since immanence is being contrasted with creation, we must again ask in what God's creative activity consists. Creation is the gradual progress, by means of sporting variation and of the tendency toward habit-taking, from chaotic nothingness to concrete reasonableness, the *summum bonum*. The deity's creative functions are to introduce the chance variations, and, as Ideal, to draw the world toward its full actuality as God's creation. By introducing chance variations, God presents the existing set of facts with new possibilities, and this God cannot be simply identified with what is. As ideal outcome of evolution, God is more than any world of mere facts, possibilities, or finite minds.

At least another brief word is in order about Peirce's treatment of the problem of evil. From 1893 on, he tended to "pooh-pooh" the problem—to use a favorite Peircean expression—and to say that Henry James, Sr. had already solved it satisfactorily. God's love, if it is to be real love, needs the defect of love, even hatefulness and hatred, as its object. (CP 6.287) Evil is even necessary to the evolutionary process: "Love, recognizing germs of loveliness in the hateful, gradually warms it into life, and makes it lovely." (CP 6.289) In the last years, however, Peirce took a renewed interest in the problem in relation to the phenomenon of pain. The evolutionary process still provided in 1907 whatever explanation is available:

> Man cannot entirely see why God inflicts pain; but he can see that pain amounts to an instinct to avoid certain feelings, and that its existence harmonizes beautifully with the general idea of the universe that ends are worked out gradually. (MS 843)

Now pain, despite our tendency to think otherwise, is nothing but feeling, neither good nor evil. Good and evil are ideas relative to ends. (MS 649) Since the development of anaesthetics, we know that many ends toward which pain was formerly thought to be an indispensable means can be achieved without it. Thus we must recognize that pain is a First, while evil is a Third. Evil then resides exclusively in the moral realm:

> ... the precise definition of Evil is 'that which man ought to fight'; so that nothing which man cannot put down can be evil, and the only things left for man to blame are those he can control; namely his own conduct and the conduct of those subject to him. (MS 843)

Thus Peirce moved from attributing evil directly to God, to seeing it in a somewhat stoic manner. How something feels is not a good indicator of its moral quality; its goodness or badness consists in its contribution to or derogation from critically chosen human purposes.

God or Reason

Perhaps the most helpful sort of conclusion to this chapter will be the examination of a few more texts, all taken from the year 1909. Each of these texts, from unpublished work, confirms my suspicion that Peirce's theism amounted to a belief that certain inescapable beliefs we all hold can be expressed in religious language when such expression is appropriate or necessary for worship and the conduct of life. An example would be a belief in the orderliness and reasonableness of Nature. I call these and similar passages Peirce's "or" locutions because they sound like Spinoza's "God or Nature" or "Substance." In the elder Peirce the analogous are "God," or "Reason," or the "Ideal," or the *summum bonum,* or "the Truth." In 1909, "Reason" was his favorite. He wrote, for example, in a letter draft to Samuel Barnett on 8 December 1909, that "the whole reasoning of science supposes that there really is a *reason* in nature into which Human Reason is a more or less imperfect insight. . . ." (MS 136; cf. MS 634) On 27 May he had described Bernard Bolzano as a man who "loving and adoring that unknown god, *the-Truth-whatever-it-may-be*. . . cannot foresee what proposition his divine master, the unknown truth, may not command him to maintain . . . ." (MS 622)

On Christmas, 1909, he wrote at least two drafts of a letter to William James. One section comments on research into communication with the dead:

> There is no solace in that kind of thing. On the other hand in the simple reflexion that the Universe is governed by Absolute Reason there is greater stimulus to a happy view than any kind of future life we can imagine would bring. (MS L224)

A final passage, dated November 1909 and entitled "Significs and Logic," is especially revealing: for Peirce, learning was a religious experience, and the community of inquirers was a kind of religious community:

> Whoever learns any truth he did not know before, and learns it not from mortal lips but from those of Reason embodied in the very objects to which that truth relates, experiences a joy, which when it has often come to him and he has well considered it, he will recognize as having a religious depth and command. If then he finds himself in possession of facilities of any kind for making discoveries in a certain line of research that no others quite share, he will be likely too impelled to devote himself to that line in the full sense of "devotion"; and other men who are devoted to lines closely akin to his own will be to him more than *brothers;* they will be his brethren. Now if, in his studies, he comes upon a concept new and valuable to them all, he ought to consider himself bound in loyalty to them and to that Reason that has been his teacher and the conferer of that joy that he knows as so deep and so high, to provide that concept with a cluster of new words in which it may be applied to new objects, and may itself be further studied . . . . (MS 641)

Peirce's own musement process had led him to see a religious significance in natural processes and especially in his own ability to learn to understand them. He had come to see the sacred in the secular (though these are not Peircean terms), because even in the processes of nature he found "more" than facts and qualitative sense-data; he found Thirdness, continuities (NEM 4: xxiv), reasonableness, intelligence. He had found, with Royce, the Infinite Absolute; he had found, in the early 1900s, the *summum bonum*; he had found, for many years, Reason (SS: 75) and reasonableness in Nature. All of these, when the context seemed appropriate, he was willing to call God.

Chapter V

REASONABLENESS

This study set out to answer three questions: (1) what was Peirce's conception of God, (2) how did it develop, (3) how integral is this conception to Peirce's scientific philosophy? Each of these questions has already been addressed more than once by way of examination of Peircean texts. It is now time to summarize the findings of this chronological study, and to conclude with some critical assessment of Peirce's contributions to philosophical theology.

Peirce's Conception of God

In Peirce's mature view, God is the element of Reason or reasonableness which both expresses itself in creating, and also is emerging in the creative process. This reasonableness is not only the ideal outcome of the evolutionary process, but is also the ideal of Peirce's three normative sciences. As esthetic ideal, reasonableness is that which is unqualifiedly admirable, the *summum bonum*. Peirce even referred to this conception of God as "esthetic theism." As ethical ideal, reasonableness is the ideal of self-controlled conduct toward which we move by means of the continual review of life Peirce advocated. As logical ideal, reasonableness is the Truth as goal of all thought and all scientific inquiry. Each of these ideals, especially the esthetic and the logical, Peirce was willing to call God under what seemed to him appropriate circumstances, that is, when the question was of worship or of the conduct of life. God as ideal is the author of all beauty, power, and thought (MS L224)—author of the three universes of experience, and of the realms of the normative sciences.

Now reasonableness, Peirce thought, is an anthropomorphic concept which, attributed to nature, amounts to personifying it. He was thus led to hypothesize the reality of a personal God and to call himself a theist. It must be recalled, however, that personhood, for Peirce was not primarily an individual matter; particular facts are Seconds, and person is a symbol, that is, a Third (CP 6.270) Thus to view God as personal is precisely to understand God as some general character of the universe, that is, its evolving reasonableness, not some individual item or collection of items either inside or outside nature. Whether such a concept of God as person gives Peirce the right to call himself a theist is still an open question. Surely both Peirce and the traditional theist will have to exhibit the pragmatic consequences of a conception of personality before this issue can be decided. Since, however, a general cannot be exhausted in any particular or set of particulars, and is never entirely embodied, God cannot be wholly immanent in nature, nor can God be finite like the deities of James and of F. C. S. Schiller.

On the contrary, God and the world are the most general of symbols and are signs of each other. The world signifies God as its ultimate interpretant, and God in turn signifies the infinite—never completely achieved—meaning of the world, of all possibility, fact, and thought. There are not two truths: there are only two signs, mutually interpretable, of the same reality: God, the Reason in nature.

Such a concept of God, according to Peirce, belongs to nearly everyone, though not everyone is aware of believing in such a deity. Many have been misled by the dogmatic attitudes of the clergy, others by the attempts of theologians to make vague beliefs precise, and still others by their own nominalism. All the same, the belief that a question has a true answer—whether this assumption be made by scientists or by ordinary people—amounts to a belief that nature is reasonable. Such belief, since it regulates conduct, is real pragmatic belief, and when sufficiently reflected upon, may become explicit. Musement upon growth in reasonableness, found in the universes of possibility, existence, or generality, will lead the muser to recognize the religious character of the implicitly held belief. In other words, what the scientist believes and what the religious person experiences and worships, is one and the same reality. The words we use to describe this reality must vary to suit the purpose of the discourse. "God" is usually an inappropriate word in philosophy, and "the Absolute" does not belong in church. The reality denoted in the two language systems is the same, even though the words are not appropriately interchangeable.

Development

How did this conception of God, with the accompanying conviction that all people implicitly possess it, develop? The project Peirce undertook in his college years and in his twenties to reform Kant's logic and to find an adequate system of categories, combined with his conviction that there are no incognizables, set him the choice of making religion reasonable, or of abandoning it. From his earliest years Peirce was unsatisfied with solutions which would postulate a scientific and philosophical truth on one side, with a religious and moral truth on the other. Faith had to be reasonable, and reason could be tested by its correspondence with faith's practical expression.

In his middle years (1867-1887), which saw the development of the pragmatic maxim and of the view that reality consists in the ultimate opinion to be reached in the long run by the community of inquirers, Peirce came to identify the object of religious belief with the truth to be discovered in scientific inquiry. In his last years he remembered having thought since the 1880s that there was a reason in nature to which our own must be akin in order for science to be possible. Such a reason he seems to have identified with "the Perfect" and "the Supreme Ideal" of his comments on Vacherot. This identification was complete enough by 1885 for him to think that it should be obvious to Royce that "the mind of God" and "the ultimate outcome of inquiry" are merely different words for the same conception.

Peirce's development of an evolutionary cosmology in the 1880s and early 1890s affected his conception of God. The ideal perfection of knowledge became the ultimate outcome of evolution, and thus was linked to an overall cosmology. The cosmos with its natural laws develops by means of the spontaneous action of chance in the chaos. Dead habit-bound matter is broken up, and new, more reasonable patterns get the opportunity to develop and survive. On those occasions when Peirce used religious language to describe this process, he called it creation, and attributed to God both the initial play of chance as well as the ultimate outcome. He was careful to say that God is *now* creating the world.

In the early 1890s, Peirce began to identify the God of religious experience (not of theologians) with both the process and the product of evolution. God is love, and love produces growth. Without religious experience, however, a person is in no way entitled to use religious language because such a person could not know what it means. Peirce was clearly troubled by the elitist implications of this view, but could not resolve the problem in the 1890s. His "neglected argument" would later suggest that the required experience is available to anyone.

By the late 1890s and early 1900s, Peirce had integrated his concept of the ultimate outcome of evolution, his final upshot of inquiry, and the concept of the *summum bonum* into an ideal of concrete reasonableness. His identification of God with each and all of these, and with reasonableness itself, makes it clear how thoroughly involved his religion had become with what he took to be natural processes: evolution, thought, and conduct.

In his last decades of writing, however, Peirce made it clear that his "theism" involved a God who is not simply identifiable with natural processes, though active and discoverable within them. God is the element of Reason in nature, but also always beyond it, as an ideal always transcends what already exists. Now ideals, for Peirce, were much more real than mere facts; they have pragmatic meaning or intellectual import. In this case, the view that nature is reasonable makes the practical activities of science reasonable and is equivalent to an implicit belief in God.

How to make this scientific belief explicit, or how to make religious experience available to everyone, was the subject of Peirce's last published article on religious topics. By a process of musement, or meditative play, a person could come to recognize the creator in the beauty and growth of the universe. Free meditation, regularly pursued, would produce recognition of one's instinctive belief in the immensely attractive idea of God. The hypothesis of God's reality, generated retroductively by musement upon the surprising facts of variety and growth, can then be seen as a case of scientific reasoning. The reasoning process continues through deduction of the idea's practical consequences, and includes checking to see if the predicated consequences—for worship and the conduct of life as well as for thought— actually occur. So God as reasonableness becomes the reasonable abductive hypothesis par excellence.

God and Peirce's Philosophy

It seems undeniable that Peirce himself thought God, under various names, was a conception required by the rest of his philosophical views. His pragmatism and theory of inquiry required an ideal truth. His synechism needed a continuum to include all continua. His normative sciences wanted the *summum bonum,* and his evolutionist cosmology, he believed, required the double Absolute, the Alpha and Omega. Each of these—the ideal truth, the Absolute, the *summum bonum,* and even the continuum—was a philosophical description of the God of religious experience and of worship.

But was his own view correct? Several possible answers to this question may be briefly examined. The first would hold that Peirce was simply a philosophical/religious split personality, naturalist and transcendentalist, tough-minded and tender-minded, empiricist and rationalist, just as the mood struck him. It seems to me that the very occurrence of much of Peirce's religious writing in scientific and mathematical contexts, his abhorrence of two-truth theories (CP 6.216), and his devotion to the architectonic ideal of philosophical system, all preclude this solution.

A second possibility, closely related to the first, is to say that Peirce was simply wrong: that ideals, truth, absolutes, reasonableness, and continua have nothing whatever to do with religion. To say this is to deny that reason and faith have anything at all to do with one another. The implications of this position are ominous: reason can no longer criticize faith's self-understanding; fundamentalism must thus prevail if any religious belief is possible; philosophy is deprived of a whole realm of experience to explain. Both religion and philosophy are thus impoverished. Above all, religious conceptions must be classed as meangingless by philosophers. There is no possibility of translation between philosophical and religious language. Either there are two truths, or no religious truth. Peirce might give at least two answers to this criticism. First, he would say that for the pragmaticist, if any two conceptions, e.g. of God, have the same conceivable practical consequences, they have the same meaning and express the same truth. Second, both religious and philosophical words are signs of the same object, the human experience each of us has every waking minute of every day. So for Peirce, the truth, the Absolute, the *summum bonum,* reasonableness, and God, are simply different interpretations of experience appropriate to various contexts; their pragmatic import is often indistinguishable. To affirm one is not to deny the others; that would be like making a mechanical explanation of how a computer works into a denial that a mind designed it or that it works in an orderly fashion. On the contrary, to believe in human reasonableness is to believe in Reason as a general character of the universe, and Peirce could imagine nothing more worthy of his reverential recognition, in other words, of his worship. It might be suggested that Occam's razor could be applied to Peirce's work: if Reason or ideals or limit concepts will do the job, why add God to the cosmos? This is to miss Peirce's point: that the ideal and reasonable character of nature is just the philosopher's way of expressing the reality that the religious instinct calls "God." To talk of a deity is not to add an item to the universe; it is to describe the totality in an additional way, one especially fruitful for the conduct of life.

Now, to see God as the general character of Reason in the world and creating the world, suggests a third way to approach the question of the relation of Peirce's theism to the rest of his philosophy, namely through his theory of categories or "phenomenology." While Peirce once said that God was Absolute First and Absolute Second, it is striking that from the beginning to the end of his life, God is most often identified with Thirdness. God is the *Thou* in the pre-1867 formulations, and later is related to, if not identified with, the order of nature, continuity, the reality of general ideals, and the most general of the signs of which logic became the science. Thus, for Peirce, if Thirdness is real, so is his philosophical conception of God. "God's essence is reality." So Peirce's "theism" stands or falls with the realism of his theory of categories. In fact, I suspect that this issue of realism is the dividing line between those who take Peirce seriously and those who do not—his religious thought included.

It might be objected that such "theism" bears scarcely any relation to that of the Judaeo-Christian tradition. In 1878 Peirce might have replied, "So much the worse for that tradition." The older Peirce would suggest that the objector had probably never reflected on the pragmatic meaning of theism, of religious experience, or of the real, all of which leads to the concept of God as love-producing reasonableness and repudiates the conduct implied by the "Gospel of Greed." The God of Peirce's categories is the most general of all general signs, and thus the most personal—a traditional anthropomorphic God. But the ultimate interpretant of a God-conception lies in its effects on conduct; if these consequences correspond to those of the traditional account—as Peirce believed they did—then any difference between the two descriptions of God is merely verbal.

Certainly it would be possible to talk of Peirce's various Thirdnesses and Ideals without making explicit reference to God; in fact he usually did so, preferring to reserve that name for special purposes and contexts. But unless the practical consequences of reasonableness and the Absolute be also removed, the conception of God has not been eliminated, and some kind of "theism" remains. I therefore think Peirce was right in believing his religious beliefs integral to his whole scientific philosophy, though their direct expression belonged to other contexts.

Critical Assessment

Several types of objections may be raised against Peirce's religious beliefs and against the uses he made of them. For example, the condition of his writings, together with the scattered and brief character of most of his utterances on religious topics might be said to make it difficult, if not impossible, to attribute to him a philosophical theology, let alone to use it as some kind of basis for systematic theology. To this criticism—which would discount Peirce as a contributor to the ongoing dialogue in Western philosophy on God's nature and reality, and which would dismiss the objectives of this present study as having no importance—at least three replies may be made. First of all, it must be granted that Peirce's writings on this topic are frustratingly enigmatic. That admitted, however, it should be remarked that the same can be said of much of the rest of Peirce's work as well. This fact has not, however, prevented contemporary philosophers from studying Peirce, and from looking to him for contributions to contemporary philosophical dialogue. In addition, Peirce saw himself as a systematic philosopher, and usually explained ideas by elucidating their connections with other ideas, so his thought is probably less disconnected than it often seems. With respect to the God-problem, the student of Peirce must admittedly read between the lines more often than one might wish, a problem which arises from Peirce's reluctance to use religious language in philosophy. Still, many interesting suggestions for approaches to the problems of philosophical theology can be found in Peirce's work; it is with the nature and worth of these suggestions that this study has been concerned. Finally, if his thought would not be regarded as helpful by systematic theologians, then Peirce probably would have found in that one more piece of evidence that their whole enterprise was just as thoroughly bankrupt as he had thought. Until theologians abandon dogmatism for the fallibilistic spirit of the scientific love of truth, they will be in no position to learn from anyone.

A more serious charge could be leveled at Peirce for failing to take the problem of evil seriously. It might be said that he, like all pantheistic monists, simply makes God the sum of what is, and thus removes the ordinary sense of the terms 'good' and 'evil'. If Peirce is to be a theist and attribute creation to God, even creative activity in the present, he needs to admit that even his critical common-sensism would regard certain phenomena as evil—incest, for example. He should ask how responsible his reasonable God is for the existence of such evils. If he does not ask such questions, the sceptic is surely right in saying that Peirce's religious assertions are nonfalsifiable, and thus lacking in cognitive significance.

It seems to me that Peirce had at least two avenues open to him for response to this very serious critique. One would be to say that God does not create the world alone, that human self-controlled conduct plays a part; and that we should expect some pain in the growth process of evolving reasonableness. These suggestions, made by Peirce in a late unpublished manuscript (MS 843) and quite in accord with the traditional emphases on human choice as cause of evil and with John Hick's soul-making world (1963: 40-42), unfortunately appear, to my knowledge, nowhere in Peirce's published work and were never much developed by him. But these suggestions could surely be developed, considering that Peirce's deity is not the sum of all existents, but rather is the ideal reasonableness that is still emerging. Like all process thinkers, Peirce requires us to rethink the traditional theistic attribute of omnipotence.

To the objection that his God-talk was nonfalsifiable, Peirce might have responded that the complete cessation of all scientific inquiry might convince him that God was not real or that God was not creating the world. Obviously he was never confronted with the nonfalsifiability criterion in its contemporary form, but since scientific inquiry, as truthseeking and reasonableness-creating, was his favorite evidence for "Reason" or God, it seems to me that he does possess a pragmatic test. Whether or not we can know that there will in fact be convergence of scientific opinion upon "the truth" in the long run, we know that scientists do conduct their lives as if there were truth to be found out, as if the unknown God, the-truth-whatever-it-may-be, were real. If scientists cease to seek knowledge, Peirce must then doubt his belief in God.

A third question to be asked of Peirce is how he knows his God is not a projection or self-deception, something he wants to believe. Peirce, consistently critical of William James's "Will to Believe," would have at least two replies. First of all, we do not choose our beliefs or create our doubts. When inquiry stops, when actual doubt ceases, we believe. We may, by musement, place ourselves in a position to experience that which would convince us, but the belief forces itself upon us if we are sufficiently reflective. We "recognize" the deity; we do not create it. In addition, Peirce would have said, by their fruits you shall know them. If a conception of God as reasonableness has its effects on the reason-seeking activities of the community of inquirers, if it expresses itself in evolutionary love of neighbor, then this conception has reality in the pragmaticistic sense. The existence of reacting Seconds Peirce never claimed for the deity; its reality, like the power of any general idea, is tested in its effects on conduct. A conception of God that sets people to fighting with each other Peirce would have called self-deception; he assumed cooperation as a positive value. When Peirce evaluated religious belief by the same criterion he used for all conceptions—the pragmatic test—he thought he minimized the probability of error.

Another sort of objection to be expected against Peirce's theism is that it rests upon a species of the design argument, and thus lies open to Hume's whole critique. In fact, Peirce himself criticized design arguments in 1878. Nature, he thought then, is just not orderly enough to justify any such inference to a designer outside the natural order. Perhaps he thought later that his "hypothetical" God, object of belief not of certainty, would satisfy even the sceptical Hume. Or perhaps he thought "reasonableness," especially since it is admittedly only gradually emerging, did not require that the order of nature be perfect but only that it be developing, manifesting a tendency towards ends. His theory would thus escape Hume's critique. Surely Peirce's God is not a blueprint maker, but rather is the design creating itself in the universe. In any case, it would surely have helped if Peirce had enlightened us further on these matters.

A final criticism of Peirce's conception of God—one to be expected from religious people—would be that his deity is described in terms too exclusively intellectual. Such a philosophical God could appeal only to the cognitive, not the affective, side of a person. Such an objection seems to miss the force of the appeal to religious experience, and ignores Peirce's talk of loving, of beauty and attractiveness, and of feeling comforted. Worst of all, it misses the passionate love of truth Peirce describes scientists as possessing. Like Plato, whose *Eros* is above all experienced in the search for truth, Peirce saw no need to divide the cognitive and the affective domains with respect to the lovableness of God. To love God as a person would be to love God as sign of the general reasonableness of nature. God can then be perceived and loved in learning as well as in human relationships. Evolution itself is a product of love for those near to us in life and feeling, and those involved with us in the search for truth; one might only wish Peirce had developed this theme more. But the search for truth need not be unfeeling. When Peirce described scientific philosophy as "passionless," I think he meant fallibilistic, non-dogmatic, uncaring for any personal gain. But the search for truth requires a commitment and dedication Peirce described as religious and thus appeals both to rationality and to feeling.

There are some positive things to be said of Peircean theism. Its best feature may be a reasonable balance of immanence and transcendence. God is not completely identified with natural processes, much less with the sum of all the items in the universe. (Only the universe of Seconds could be regarded as such a collection, and it has no independent reality.) Rather, the divine is the tendency, manifested in natural processes, of growth toward reasonableness. Thus, God's creative activity is seen as thoroughly immanent, operating by means of chance, and through natural growth.

But the deity also transcends the world, just as the truth transcends the search for it, and as ideal perfection escapes the striving for it. "The Absolute" expresses Peirce's view that God is beyond the merely actual, and though not incognizable, neither is God fully known. Thus a student of

Peirce is not asked to choose among the alternatives of a crude pantheism, deism with its utterly remote divinity, and agnosticism or atheism. A Peircean theist has a God describable in religious terms as loving and adorable creator and governor of the universe, but understandable philosophically as *summum bonum* both beyond and emerging within the world. As a result, God may never be fully captured within our explanations, but yet does not belong to some realm of "incognizable" noumena.

Secondly, I think Peirce deserves some credit for the recognition that the God of his theism is "strictly hypothetical." (CP 6.467) There are two ways this "strictly" could be taken: as "nothing but" or as "speaking scientifically, not religiously." Because Peirce often said that we have practical certainty with regard to our actual beliefs, I lean toward the second interpretation. Even if he meant "nothing but" hypothetical, his explanation of the testability of the retroductive hypothesis, "whose ultimate test must lie in its value in the self-controlled growth of man's conduct of life" (CP 6.480), shows that this particular hypothesis is supposed to have an immense practical impact upon its believers. But false beliefs can also have a great impact, so we must still hold all beliefs as hypotheses in a fallibilistic spirit.

The great advantage of a "hypothetical" God is to keep the believer intellectually honest. No matter how plausible and attractive a believer may find a religious view of the world, one who holds all beliefs lightly will always be ready to notice a "surprising fact" which might require the revision or rejection of the believed hypothesis. As noted above, Peirce would probably recognize the cessation of all scientific inquiry as such a "surprising fact." So such a theist is not open to the charge of holding nonfalsifiable beliefs. Development of this kind of theism might add a whole new set of possibilities to contemporary philosophical theology, as well as a new set of questions about faith for philosophy of religion.

Another contribution Peircean theism might make to current discussion lies in the area of religious language (Orange, 1983). At present the options seem to be: (1) religious statements, according to Antony Flew, are empty or meaningless because neither verifiable nor falsifiable (1955: 96-99); (2) religious statements, for R. M. Hare, are not assertions, but "bliks" or uncritically held presuppositions which determine the interpretation of all experience, and are thus nonfalsifiable, at least for the believer (Flew, 1955: 99-103); (3) religious assertions, in Basil Mitchell's view, do not lead to clear predictions, and are thus not clearly falsifiable (Flew, 1955: 103-105); (4) religious statements can only be verified in the future, eschatologically (Crombie, 1957: 31-83). All of these positions amount to the view that religious language is nonscientific, and if it has any meaning at all, this meaning resembles that of poetry or of mythology. In other words, religious language is merely metaphorical and has no precisely assignable cognitive significance. Were Peirce here today, he would probably object that certain beliefs, even among those held by scientists, are intrinsically vague. No scientist believes nature is entirely capricious, but one would be hard-pressed to explain definitely what belief in its orderliness consists in. In addition, scientists make use of all sorts of theoretical concepts and entities, whose real existence is neither verifiable nor falsifiable. They are simply highly useful and plausible. Why should philosophy demand more rigor from religion than it does from science?

Peirce would also suggest that not all religious language has the same cognitive status. In addition to discriminating degrees of literal or metaphorical character, he would distinguish the central religious belief from the dogmatic statements of creeds produced by the *odium theologicum,* the desire to exclude someone from the church. In addition, he would say that most statements about historical events or their interpretation are not worth arguing about because we have so little reliable evidence about them. So, he would say, let us restrict the discussion to statements like "God is love," "God is creator," and "God governs the universe." Exactly the same problems of religious language arise with respect to these assertions, so there is no need to complicate the question by adding statements from the creeds or traditions of particular churches.

Peirce's distinctive contribution to the religious language problem probably lies in his sign-theory, or semiotic. Every sign has an interpretant, another sign produced in the interpreter. The task of the analysis of religious language is to provide pragmatic guidelines for interpretation. In part, such guidelines take the form of a cosmology within which all particular assertions do or do not make sense. Just as a logician provides a dictionary for symbols employed, a cosmologist provides a system of interpretation for signs of possibilities, facts, and general ideas within the universe, and Peirce gave at least sketchy definitions of terms at the beginning of his "Neglected Argument." Now Peirce's theistic speculation can be seen as an attempt to do just this: to show how God-talk can be translated into world-talk, transcendentalism into naturalism, and vice versa, without loss of meaning, and without dividing truth into "two warring factions." So Peirce's religious language is no more or less meaningful, he would say, than the rest of his scientific philosophy. It is simply a question of appropriate contexts. This is not anthropological, but rather Aristotelian, relativism.

A hard-line positivist would reject all of Peirce's phenomenology and cosmology as so much "metaphysics," and his religious view along with them. Peirce would then launch into a tirade against the positivist's nominalism, and the battle would be joined. But in dialogue with any milder view, the suggestion that religious language can be interpreted into naturalistic language, and vice versa, and that its meaning consists in its conceivable effects upon conduct, may add a fresh dimension to the discussion of the cognitive status of religious language. "By their fruits you shall know them," Peirce liked to quote. Without fruits, religious language would be worse than empty; it would be hypocritical.

In summary, it is probably fair to say that many difficulties in assessing Peirce's contributions to philosophical theology, and in determining the exact character of his deity, do stem from the brevity of his writings on the topic. He never produced his book on religion of which he often spoke in his last years. Still, he provided both helpful criticism of other views, an example of the approach to these questions in a scientific spirit, and an affirmation of a more or less traditional transcendence-and-immanence theism in terms which commended themselves to an "Exact Logician."

If the reader of Peirce wishes to take his phenomenology and cosmology in completely naturalistic terms, and to ignore the religious interpretation he gave to his thought, the reader will not be completely wrong, even for Peirce, but (as he said) "it will not give me a high opinion of your intelligence." (CP 6.489)

REFERENCES

Boler, J. *Charles Peirce and Scholastic Realism.* Seattle: University of Washington Press, 1963.

Buzzelli, D. The 'New List of Categories': A Study in the Early Philosophy of Charles Sanders Peirce. (Doctoral dissertation, Fordham University, 1974).

Clarke, B. L. Peirce's Neglected Argument. *Transactions of the Charles S. Peirce Society,* 1977, *13,* 277-287.

Crombie, I. The Possibility of Theological Statements. *Faith and Logic,* ed. B. Mitchell. London: George Allen and Unwin, 1957.

Flew, A. and MacIntyre, A. *Theology and Falsification.* New York: Macmillan, 1955.

Fisch, M. H. Hegel and Peirce. *Proceedings of the 1972 Hegel Society of America.* The Hague: Martinus Nijhoff, 1974.

Fisch, M. H. Peirce's Progress from Nominalism toward Realism. *Monist,* 1967, *51,* 159-178.

Fisch, M. H. Peirce's Arisbe: The Greek Influence in His Later Philosophy. *Transactions of the Charles S. Peirce Society,* 1971, *7,* 187-210.

Harrison, S. Man's Glassy Essence. Doctoral dissertation, Fordham University, 1971.

Hick, J. *Philosophy of Religion.* Englewood Cliffs: Prentice-Hall, 1963.

James, H. Sr. *Substance and Shadow.* Boston: Ticknor and Fields, 1863.

James, H. Jr. *Notes of a Son and Brother.* New York: Scribners, 1914.

James, W. *The Will to Believe and other Essays in Popular Philosophy.* New York: Longmans Green, 1897.

Ketner, K. L. Peirce's Ethics of Terminology. *Transactions of the Charles S. Peirce Society,* 1981, *17,* 327--347.

Krolikowski, W. The Peircean Vir. In *Studies in the Philosophy of Charles Sanders Peirce,* second series. Ed. E. Moore and R. S. Robin. Amherst: University of Massachusetts Press, 1964.

Lauer, Q. Hegel's Pantheism. *Thought,* 1979, *44,* 5-23.

Mansel, H. L. *The Limits of Religious Thought,* third edition. London: John Murray, 1859.

Mahowald, M. Peirce's Concepts of God and Religion. *Transactions of the Charles S. Peirce Society,* 1976, *12,* 367-377.

Michael, E. Peirce on Individuals. *Transactions of the Charles S. Peirce Society,* 1976, *12,* 321-329.

Murphey, M. G. *The Development of Peirce's Philosophy.* Cambridge: Harvard University Press, 1961.

Orange, D. Peirce and Falsification. *American Journal of Semiotics,* 1983, *2,* 121-127.

Perry, R. B. *The Thought and Character of William James.* 2 vols. Boston: Little, Brown, 1935.

Potter, V. G. *Charles S. Peirce on Norms and Ideals.* Amherst: University of Massachusetts Press, 1967.

Potter, V. G. "Vaguely like a Man": The Theism of Charles S. Peirce. In *God Knowable and Unknowable.* Ed. R. J. Roth. New York: Fordham University Press, 1973.

Potter, V. G. C. S. Peirce's Argument for God's Reality: A Pragmatist's View. In *The Papin Festschrift: Essays in Honor of Joseph Papin,* ed. J. Armenti. Villanova: Villanova University Press, 1976.

Potter, V. G. and Shields, P. Peirce's Definitions of Continuity. *Transactions of the Charles S. Peirce Society,* 1977, *13,* 20-34.

Royce, J. *The Religious Aspect of Philosophy.* Boston: Houghton Mifflin, 1885.

Royce, J. *The World and the Individual,* 2 vols. New York: Macmillan, 1899 and 1901.

Schiller, F. *On the Aesthetic Education of Man.* Trans. R. Snell. New York: Ungar, 1954.

Scott, F. J. Peirce and Schiller and their Correspondence. *Journal of the History of Philosophy,* 1973, *11,* 363-386.

Smith, J. E. *Purpose and Thought.* New Haven: Yale University Press, 1978.

Smith, T. *Revivalism and Social Reform.* New York: Harper, 1957.

Swedenborg, E. *Love and Wisdom.* Trans. J. C. Ager. New York: Swedenborg Foundation, 1976.

Trammell, R. L. Religion, Instinct, and Reason in the Thought of Charles S. Peirce. *Transactions of the Charles S. Peirce Society,* 1972, *8,* 3-25.

Trammel, R. L. Charles Sanders Peirce and Henry James the Elder. *Transactions of the Charles S. Peirce Society,* 1973, *11,* 202-220.

Vacherot, E. *La Religion.* Paris: Librairie Chamerot, 1869.

Wiener, P. ed. *Values in a Universe of Chance.* Garden City: Doubleday, 1958.